Indonesian Fighting
Fundamentals

Indonesian Fighting Fundamentals

The Brutal Arts of the Archipelago

BOB ORLANDO

PALADIN PRESS • BOULDER, COLORADO

Also by Bob Orlando:
Fighting Arts of Indonesia (video)
Reflex Action (video)
Fighting Footwork of Kuntao-Silat (video and workbook)
Fighting Forms of Kuntao-Silat (DVD & workbook)

ABOUT THE COVER

The two flags represent the nations of Indonesia and the Netherlands. Indonesia's contribution to the body of martial arts is considerable, and this book is about principles extracted from the arts practiced there. The tricolor Dutch flag is present because Dutch-Indonesian masters remain Indonesia's best martial art ambassadors. Moreover, their contribution to Indonesia's indigenous arts is both unique and significant—a rare blend of East and West.

The *garuda*, or eagle, holding the traditional Indonesian *tjabang*, or truncheons, is similar to insignias used by several Dutch-Indonesian teachers. As such, it is emblematic of their skill and the arts they represent.

Indonesian Fighting Fundamentals:
The Brutal Arts of the Archipelago
by Bob Orlando

Copyright © 1996 by Bob Orlando

ISBN 13: 978-0-87364-892-9
Printed in the United States of America

Published by Paladin Press, a division of
Paladin Enterprises, Inc., P.O. Box 1307,
Boulder, Colorado 80306, USA.
(303) 443-7250

Direct inquiries and/or orders to the above address.

Visit our website at www.paladin-press.com

Garuda symbol copyrighted by Bob Orlando
Cover and Illustrations by Michael Dolcé
Photographs by Roy A. Sorenson

Contents

Contents

To My Best Friend

My greatest source of human help and encouragement is my wife, Terry. No one should have to listen to and read all of the drafts my sweet wife has had to endure. Despite this, at every reading her willingness to help has remained steadfast. As I see it, she has worked harder for this book than I have, for she often relieves me of household chores so that I am not distracted from writing.

Many a talented individual has been forced to end his walk down the martial path because his wife has not understood the drive and the dedication such a course requires. Through all these years, my wife has done more than simply tolerate my dedication to the mistress I call my art; she has steadfastly helped and encouraged me every step of the way. Her contributions and support to my life are, and continue to be, incalculable, and any credit I may receive as a man or a martial artist must be shared with her.

Foreword

In the past 30 years, a myriad of martial art "how-to" books have appeared on the shelves of local bookstores. As with most physical subjects, it is exceedingly difficult (if even possible) to learn a martial art from a book. *Indonesian Fighting Fundamentals* does not attempt to teach you *how* to do martial arts. However, it does—and this is an important distinction—examine and explain *why* basic combat principles of Indonesian fighting arts are so effective.

Bob Orlando's nearly three decades of martial art training are a case study in applying analytical skills to Indonesia's highly effective fighting arts. But simply saying that Bob has applied analytical skills to these arts is a gross understatement. In my 30+ years as a student and teacher of martial arts, rarely have I met an individual who can, in a few seconds, observe and distill what takes the rest of us hundreds of repetitions to comprehend. His is a rare gift and one that benefits us all.

Although Bob is not the first American to learn these arts, he is the first to recognize, distill, and document commonalities found in these combat systems. Pragmatic in his approach, Bob has done more than simply mimic the techniques and movements taught to him. He has questioned, explored, and analyzed everything he was shown. More than that, he has formulated drills that ingrain these fundamental principles into his students, and he has organized the training methodologies into a format that martial artists at all levels of expertise can understand and apply.

Indonesian Fighting Fundamentals: The Brutal Arts of the Archipelago brings amazing clarity to the previously hidden principles underlying Indonesia's fighting arts. They are not the latest "fad" in martial arts. The principles shared here have always worked and, if understood and properly applied, will continue to work in any age. If you are looking for more than just techniques, then this book is for you.

—Stewart Lauper
Progressive Martial Arts

Preface

Indonesian martial arts have only recently caught on in the United States. Those offering instruction today in those arts are largely Dutch-Indonesians: men who lived in Indonesia before the island nation gained her independence from the Netherlands in 1949. Dutch-Indonesian masters bring a rare perspective to Asian martial arts. Their unique cross-cultural heritage gives them the ability to see the arts they received through both Eastern and Western eyes.

Many of the arts Dutch-Indonesian masters learned are still taught in Indonesia; however, they are not taught—either in context or content—the same way they were taught to these men. In the last 45 years Indonesia has moved from being one of the poorest nations to one that now enjoys an unprecedented degree of prosperity. However, as in other Asian nations experiencing similar economic growth, those skilled in effective and often brutal fighting arts become anachronisms—men whose skills are now frowned upon as either uncivilized or excessively violent.

Indonesian Fighting Fundamentals: The Brutal Arts of the Archipelago examines the tactics, techniques, and methods of movement found in the arts these men learned. The focus is primarily on pentjak silat as it was practiced in colonial (World War II and preindependence) Indonesia. Chinese kuntao is discussed to a lesser degree, but both arts are addressed because the interaction and interplay between them contributed more to the overall effectiveness of Indonesian and Chinese fighting skill than either of them have independent of the other.

There are several reasons why both arts (including the closely guarded Chinese kuntao) were available to Dutch and Dutch-Indonesian practitioners. Pentjak silat, for example, was often shared with the Dutch because they married into the Indonesian community—it would be a heartless Indonesian grandfather or uncle who would not teach his grandchildren, nephews, and nieces just because they had colonial blood. Doubtless, some offered their knowledge to their Dutch overlords to curry favor, repay a debt, or show gratitude. Whatever the case, the end result was that many of the Dutch (and their children) learned pentjak silat—and a handful of them even managed to study kuntao.

But the Dutch experience in learning these Indonesian arts was significantly different from the national Indonesians' in one respect: the Dutch often had access to many different systems or styles of silat. As part of the colonial establishment, Dutch-Indonesians were never really seen as fully Indonesian. This, however, worked in their favor. Teachers who would not normally share their skills with one from another village or school often freely taught the Dutch.

In those days, protecting your martial secrets provided a measure of personal security and gave you a certain status in your community. However, from the Indonesian perspective, sharing their secrets with the Dutch was acceptable. The Dutch, they felt, played on a different field, so sharing one's skills with them did not pose the same threat as divulging them to another Indonesian might—someone who might someday challenge you.

There was much less intermarriage between the Dutch and the Chinese (the Chinese, even today, are a very close community). There was, therefore, less of a willingness on the part of the Chinese to share their arts. However, they did make exceptions. Like the Indonesians, the Chinese also saw the Dutch as playing on a different field, so it was possible for them to accept Dutch and Dutch-Indonesian children as students. Besides, as an immigrant community in a host country, it couldn't hurt to have (potentially) influential friends among the colonial establishment. Their Eurasian heritage and sociopolitical position allowed Dutch-Indonesians much greater access to both Indonesian and Chinese arts than either natural Indonesians or Chinese.

Indonesian Fighting Fundamentals: The Brutal Arts of the Archipelago analyzes arts from Indonesia's colonial period. It isolates the arts' underlying principles and outlines training methods that turn the principles into skills. But remember this: although this book is about basic combat principles inherent in Indonesian fighting arts from the colonial period, it cannot cover all the principles or all the different systems. It is impossible for anyone to detail all the characteristics, even the fundamental ones, in a single book; such an undertaking would require volumes.

Furthermore, although the book's focus is on Indonesian arts, other Southeast Asian influences are incorporated. This is because no art, nation, or culture—no one part of the world, Eastern or Western—has everything the modern martial artist needs. Every art emphasizes and offers its own unique skills. Some cultures, for example, have developed systems based exclusively on long-range fighting tactics. Others prefer grappling. Still others major in personal weaponry. All, however, contribute to the body of martial art knowledge.

I include influences from these other arts to accomplish two goals: acclimation and assimilation. Acclimation is the elevation of existing skills to a level that allows us to understand and appreciate the tactics and principles shown. For example, when I began studying Indonesian arts, I already had several years of experience and training in Chinese systems. However, little of my previous experience prepared me for what I was to learn. My eyes simply were unaccustomed to the new level of sophistication. Acclimation was necessary.

Assimilation, the second goal, is using existing training methods and developing drills and tools that help us bring the fighting principles found in Indonesian arts into our repertoire. This I call the "peanut brittle" training method. The tactics, skills, and principles derived from the Indonesian arts are the peanuts: delightful nuggets, round, robust, and full of flavor. The brittle, the flavorful sauce that binds it together, is a combination of very effective training methods found in other Southeast Asian cultures. Each complements the other, and together they produce marvelous works of art.

This book is intended primarily for the martial art student (of any rank) whose main reason for training and study is effective self-defense. One may study the martial arts for reasons other than self-defense: exercise, health, cultural interest, sport, and artistic endeavor. I study primarily for self-defense, but I find sufficient exercise in my training to keep me healthy, ample cultural interest to broaden my thinking, and enough sport and artistic expression to keep me excited and appreciative of the beauty within the art.

Whatever other benefits my training and study may provide, my primary motivation remains "effective self-defense." If this is your motivation as well, then welcome, friend, and may this book benefit you as much as my discovery of the principles described here has benefited me.

Acknowledgments

No one writes a book alone. Although one may be the author, many contribute to the effort. As I consider the help I have received, several people come to mind as having contributed, in one way or another, to this book's existence. Whatever credit I may receive for this work then, must be shared.

Since this book is about Indonesian fighting arts, credit must be given to my instructor, Willem de Thouars. Although his students address him as "Uncle," this man allows me to call him "Bill" (this does not mean that I am his equal). In my time with him, Bill has shared much more with me than just his native arts of pentjak silat and kuntao; he has also given me his very heart and soul. I call him "Bill," but in my heart, he is family—a real Dutch "Uncle." Willem de Thouars epitomizes the martial art "master" because he refers to everyone but himself as such. He often says that this individual or that is a "master in his own art." He even extends this compliment to those who have abused his friendship. For himself, however, he says only that he has some skills. (In his culture, martial artists trained to survive—not for rank.)

Two more I must mention—Mr. Stewart Lauper and Mr. George Morin. Although not my formal teachers, Stewart and George have taught me volumes. Stewart Lauper is, pound-for-pound, the toughest man I know. Moreover, inside his 145-pound frame beats a heart as generous and big as any you will ever meet. George Morin is a technician, par excellence. His movement and fluidity are the envy of many—certainly of me. As a training partner, he has seemingly infinite patience. If, as a martial artist, I have any skill, it is due in large part to each of these outstanding martial artists.

Finally, while many have contributed in one way or another to this work, one deserves special recognition for his help: Mr. Edward "Dan" Daniels. Dan is a brutal editor. He is also the one man who knows my writing style and my feelings about the art better than anyone. Like myself, Dan is a "full-time" martial artist. His occupation keeps him on the road much of the time; however, despite this, he still manages to find the time to do a number on my writing. I am fortunate that he is my friend (if he were an enemy, his cutting and slashing would be worse than murder). As a friend, Dan is the first one I call on for review and reality check—in my writing and in my art.

Notes to the Reader

Many techniques are shown in this book. The techniques were selected not because they are necessarily the best techniques for self-defense, but because they provide the best visual demonstration of the principles presented.

* * *

Like China, Indonesia has "updated" her language since gaining her independence from Dutch colonial rule. Because of this, some words are spelled two ways today (e.g., *tjimande* vs. *cimande* and *pentjak* vs. *pencak*). Although I am familiar with both spellings, for the most part, I will use the colonial spellings like *pentjak*, because these are the ones the majority of the Dutch-Indonesian teachers are the most comfortable with. (The colonial translation *pentjak* and the modern *pencak* are both pronounced pen-CHAAK.) However, even among Dutch-Indonesian masters, there is a mixing of old and new. This means that you will see the newer *pukulan* instead of the colonial *poekoelan*. (Quotations from other writers will always use their spelling.)

* * *

Finally, a word about training attire or uniforms. The uniforms worn by Dutch-Indonesian masters vary widely. Some instructors wear sarongs and other traditional Indonesian dress. Others prefer something more like the typical karate uniform. Still others teach and train in modern sweat suits, wearing the latest training shoes. The point is that there is no one "official" uniform among teachers of Indonesian arts. If you train with any instructor, wear whatever he requires. Since my instructor prefers a Colorado or Denver Broncos T-shirt, work pants, and tennis shoes, his students are free to adopt whatever uniform they wish. For this reason, you will not see me or the other participants in the technical sequences wearing anyone's idea of a traditional Indonesian martial art uniform.

Introduction

An introduction tells the reader what a book is about. Equally important is what a book is *not* about. Let me begin there.

This book is not an academic dissertation detailing the history, culture, or many fighting systems of Indonesia. One would be hard pressed to create a work that exceeds the late Donn Draeger's *Weapons and Fighting Arts of Indonesia* (Draeger 1992). His is the definitive Western work on Indonesian fighting arts and is "must" reading for anyone interested in Indonesia's martial history and culture.

Instead of detailing those things that distinguish individual pentjak silat systems from each other, *Indonesian Fighting Fundamentals: The Brutal Arts of the Archipelago* identifies general characteristics of Indonesia's fighting arts as a whole. Common attributes and characteristics are explored and examined in detail to give you an understanding of how Indonesian fighting arts differ from other Asian combat systems.

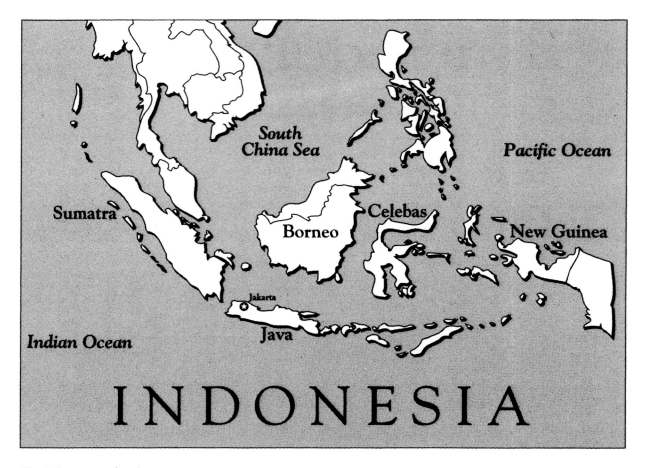

The Indonesian archipelago.

DEFINITION OF TERMS

Some of the characteristics and principles we explore have names like *adhesion*, *whiplash*, *gyroscopic rotation*, and *shearing*. Experienced martial artists (including those acquainted with Indo-Chinese arts) will likely not recognize all of these terms. They are new. My instructor rarely provided names for the attributes, characteristics, and principles inherent in the arts he taught. His teaching method was largely a "do this" approach. Details bored him. With more than half a century in the arts, he had little need for names or descriptions.

Most of the Indonesian terms I received related more to specific movements within techniques than they did to principles. The terms I learned were words like *putar kapala* (turning the head), *sempok* and *depok* (cross-legged, ground-sitting positions [figs. 1 through 3]),[1] and *beset* (rearward sweeping action [figs. 4 and 5]). Most of those technical expressions were easily remembered, and since they were more concise than English equivalents, we adopted them. However, with one exception, all of the principles and observable distinguishing characteristics described here were received without names or descriptions. Since labeling the principles was pivotal to my understanding them, I chose terms that were visually descriptive, concise, and from the language I am most comfortable with: English.

Figure 1: The *sempok* begins from a standing position.

Figure 2: The silat fighter lowers himself into the seated position.

Figure 3: Seated, but still protected.

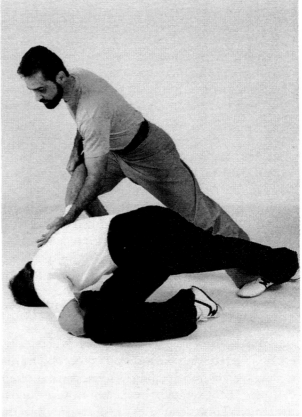

Figure 4: *Beset:* off-balancing before sweep.

Figure 5: Rearward sweeping action.

3

Other terms that may need contextual definition are *movement, motion, strategy,* and *tactic.* Although movement and motion have very similar definitions, I use them to differentiate the basic components of fighting techniques. *Movement* involves stances and how to move from position to position smoothly—left, right, off-of-center, spinning, and so on. *Motion,* on the other hand, reflects direction and action. How one strikes with elbows, from this angle or that, is motion. Since there is only the finest distinction between movement and motion, I often use one word to encompass them both: *movements.*

Strategic Versus Tactical

In the context of martial art study, a given principle may be applied strategically, tactically, or both. Applied strategically, the principle represents the grand scheme, the overarching plan for employing any number of martial skills. Tactically, it is the method used to accomplish a strategic objective. For example, the first principle we will explore (in Chapter 2) is *adhesion.* As part of an overall fight strategy, adhesion means sticking to your opponent. You allow no distance or gap between you and your attacker. Tactically, your strikes may also adhere to your opponent. For instance, instead of pulling back or rechambering the striking weapon after a blow, you might keep your hand or arm at or near the point of contact. This is an example of the tactical application of the adhesion principle. Strategic and tactical adhesion are discussed at length in Chapter 2, but for the moment, this level of understanding of those terms should be sufficient to forestall confusion.

PURE INDONESIAN ARTS

This book is not about "pure" Indonesian arts; nor is it about contemporary arts—that is, arts as they are practiced in Indonesia today. My instruction in Indonesian fighting arts comes largely from Dutch-Indonesian masters. Because of their Eurasian heritage, these men provide a unique perspective on the arts of the Indonesian archipelago—one that is, in many ways, very different from those practicing their ancestral arts in the island nation today.

This Eurasian perspective on Indonesia's fighting arts provides a natural bridge between two distant and dissimilar cultures. They are as much Dutch as they are Indonesian. They recognize the value of the Asian martial legacy they inherited, but they do so in a way that acknowledges the pragmatic realism of an "Indiana Jones."[2]

If the Dutch-Indonesian perspective is unique, so too is the opportunity my generation has to learn from them. Dutch-Indonesians represent the end of an era. With the end of Dutch colonial rule nearly 50 years ago and the rise of Indonesian nationalism, Dutch immigration to those paradisaical islands ceased. This effectively ended the social and cultural unions that occurred between these two very different peoples. Dutch-Indonesian masters are, quite literally, the last generation of their kind. As such, our opportunity to train with them is a once-in-a-lifetime occurrence. The generations of martial artists who follow us will not be as fortunate.

FROM DIFFICULTY TO DISCOVERY

Indonesian Fighting Fundamentals is about discovery. As such, it addresses the difficulties encountered during the discovery process. The difficulties are important because although difficulty is usually seen as an impediment to progress, it often turns out to be the key that unlocks the door to real discovery. For example, the Americas were discovered only after significant difficulty and hardship were overcome. This exemplifies the universal truth that "nothing that is worth anything is ever easy."

Surprisingly, the difficulties I encountered were not the usual language barriers or cultural

The Americas were discovered by ordinary men who overcame extraordinary difficulties.

impediments common to many Asian martial art programs. I was not, for example, required to learn a foreign language or the rituals and habits of another distant culture. On the contrary, I was free to absorb or reject those elements as I wished. Rather, the major difficulties stemmed from the lack of any organized or structured teaching method and the egocentricity manifested among some of the more prominent Dutch-Indonesian masters.

For example, the forms[3] I learned from Willem de Thouars were taught almost randomly with no apparent connection between them. I learned later (from some of my instructor's earlier students)[4] that there was a loose progression in the forms he taught; however, consensus among his students could only be reached on the first three forms, and that only regarding their order of introduction—not how they were performed.

Especially frustrating was the fact that when a form was taught, although it was shown several times, no two presentations were ever the same. Judging from conversations with students of other Southeast Asian masters of my instructor's generation, this method of instruction appears to be common. It is often the student, then, who decides which version he will practice.

Prearranged and ordered self-defense techniques were never taught.[5] In each lesson or class, the same attack was defended or countered spontaneously, on the spot, with no forethought or preparation. The defense might be similar to one used before, or completely different. However, it was never "punch-counter number one, two, or three."

Finally, few explanations (or at least suitable explanations) were offered regarding the application or purpose of particular movements. In recent years this situation has improved, but too late to help some earlier trainees. Judging by their explanations of the various movements and techniques contained in the forms they learned, more than a few of my instructor's early pupils have a poor understanding of his forms' applications. Each of those students, in his own way, can mimic his teacher's form, but the understanding of a given form's application and the ability to share that understanding with others are another matter.

My instructor's latter students, like myself, are not immune to these difficulties either. Understanding a movement's application and discerning its underlying principles are only slightly less arduous for us. Our interpretations and understanding are in a state of continual revision. Consequently, I tell my students that a given interpretation is an *E pluribus unum* interpretation—one of many. Furthermore, I reserve the right to change my interpretation of any movement as my knowledge grows and my understanding increases.

If lack of structure is a problem, so too is overstructuring. For all the problems in the unstructured, "catch-as-catch-can" method, the overstructured or micromanaged approach is fraught with its own share of difficulties. I remember, for example, being shown one technique that was broken down into practically baby steps. Each movement was barely inches from the one before. The technique dragged through more than a dozen steps before it was over. Majoring in the minutia of any movement is a myopic approach to instruction, and teaching this way often causes the student to lose sight of the movement's objective. At least in the unstructured approach one is kept well aware of the desired result—even if some of the detail is lost.

These teaching methods represent the extremes of the instruction spectrum; many fine Dutch-Indonesian instructors share their skill well in logical and well-ordered training programs. However, these extremes are described to give you an idea of what motivated me to dig deeper, to question everything, and to develop tools that would help me learn and practice my instructor's formidable skills. Like a miner working in a diamond mine, I recognized the value of the rough, uncut gems before me. However, merely recognizing a gem, or even possessing it, was not enough. I wanted to know how to cut and polish it for myself.

The instruction I received presented for me some very real difficulties. However, it is my belief that those difficulties led to personal discovery of the principles described in this book. If I had been given the answers—even poor answers—I might have never looked deeper. In my case, then, the difficulties led to rewarding discovery.

Bear in mind that what is presented here is incomplete. For myself, the knowledge continues to grow, now almost daily. The principles are, again, general and cut across many fighting systems practiced in Indonesia. They are basic. As such, they have great value because in any system, the advanced, more sophisticated techniques are often little more than different applications of previously learned basics; more refined, perhaps, but rarely significantly different. Learn the basics and continue to practice them with an eye to their potential, and refinement must follow.

The Value of Difficulty

It is well said that "difficulties strengthen the mind, as labor does the body."[6] That statement is as true today as it was two millennia ago. The very things that frustrated my training and study drove me to a better understanding of the principles involved. They challenged me to develop training methods that would ingrain the underlying principles into my reflexes and personal skills.

However, as much as I have benefited from this quest, I believe that my students have gained more. The drills we developed together (and I could not have done it without them) help them recognize and understand, more quickly than I, how fascinating and effective these principles from the archipelago really are.

All of this should give you a good idea of what this book is *not* about. You should have a fair idea about my perspective and a hint about the arts we'll explore. Let's look now at what this book *is* about: principles.

PRINCIPLES—FUNDAMENTAL TRUTHS

I remember reading an article in a British martial art magazine about a pentjak silat practitioner there. The gentleman in question spoke of developing spontaneity from structure and of discovering the principles behind the art. Developing spontaneity from structure (or, as my students and I like to put it, "spontaneity by rote") and discovering the principles behind the art are precisely what this book is about. To me, this is different from learning the concepts[7] of an art.

"Concepts" is a popular term that martial artists hear a lot today. According to the *Random House Dictionary of the English Language*, by definition, a concept is:

- a general notion or idea; conception
- an idea of something formed by mentally combining all of its characteristics or particulars; a construct
- a directly conceived or intuited object of thought

Those teaching concepts include many of the underlying principles in their instruction. Indeed, one cannot teach concepts without teaching the principles that support them. Concept instructors help martial artists learn the basic tenets of other systems and arts without having to spend a lifetime in each. For the advanced student, concept instruction is an excellent way to broaden his perspective and pick up technical "tricks." However, what I am sharing in this book are principles and not concepts.

I emphasize the distinction between principles and concepts because, to me, principles are more fundamental than concepts. Principles (and specifically principles of movement and motion) are the foundation on which all fighting arts are built. Concepts, on the other hand, capture general notions, ideas, and practices of an art (which may or may not include principles). For a better idea of this difference, let's look at the dictionary definition of "principle," as follows:

- an accepted or professed rule of action or conduct
- a fundamental, primary, or general law or truth from which others are described: the principle of modern physics
- a fundamental doctrine or tenet

The second definition captures the essence I am after: a principle is a fundamental, primary, general law or truth *from which others* are described. Principles give us the microview of the movement—the closer look. Concepts, on the other hand, give us the macroview—the big picture. A concept pulls together the principles and, in the process, constructs the big picture. Both views are necessary.

Applied Martially

One may learn a hand technique as part of a concept and still miss the underlying principles. Take a simple clear-and-punch maneuver where the left hand slaps down and clears the arm a fraction of a second before the right fist strikes the opponent's face (fig. 6). The concept of clearing and striking in near-simultaneous combination is familiar to many martial artists; however, a very useful underlying principle in the action is largely overlooked.

Consider the placement of the clearing hand. Place the clearing hand near the opponent's hand and farther away from his elbow, and the motion easily clears away the opponent's arm (fig. 7). Closeness to the opponent's hand provides better leverage for the clearing action. This is useful as far as it goes, but there is greater benefit in placing the left hand at or near the opponent's elbow. That done, the same

Figure 6: The left hand clearing at mid-forearm with simultaneous right punch.

Figure 7: Clearing near opponent's hand.

Figure 8: Clearing near opponent's elbow.

clearing motion now pulls the opponent into the defender's punch, thereby accelerating the target (his face) to the already onrushing punch (fig. 8).

When compared with a punch that makes full use of hip and shoulder torque, this punching technique admittedly delivers less impact to the target. But target-to-the-weapon acceleration (gained by slapping the arm down near the attacker's elbow) improves the effectiveness of even a less-than-optimal blow. There is, however, still more to be gained here. Understanding the principle behind the pulling motion in the clearing action allows us to apply it in many other ways.

The clearing action pulled the opponent into the punch precisely because it lacked the leverage to clear away the arm (leverage that was available when the clearing hand's placement was nearer the opponent's hand). Snagging the arm near the elbow bent or buckled the opponent's arm (fig. 9). This gives the defender an angle on the arm that allows him to pull the opponent and bring his head into range. You can see the usefulness of this pulling-at-the-elbow principle when facing a tall opponent.

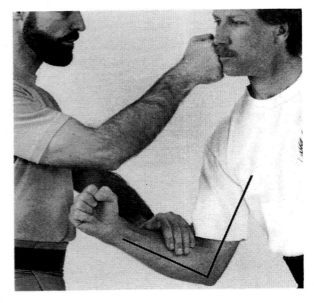

Figure 9: Close-up of the left clearing hand pulling on an arm that is bent at a true 90-degree angle.

Figure 10: Initial check.   **Figure 11:** Striking opponent's face.   **Figure 12:** Right horizontal elbow to opponent's chest.

In any fight, the head is always a prime target. It may not be easy to reach, but it remains, nonetheless, a prime target. The trick is to bring the head within range of the weapon. In the next technique, I use the pulling-at-the-elbow principle to bring the opponent's head within range. Only this time I do it not with a hand, but with an elbow.

Against a right "haymaker" punch, the defender steps inside the incoming blow. In a one-two combination, the defender intercepts the blow with his right hand and delivers a stinging left palm strike to his opponent's face (figs. 10 and 11). Since the defender has a sizable height disadvantage, he chooses to deliver a strong horizontal elbow strike to his opponent's body (fig. 12). Although this lowers his opponent's head, it is still not close enough. One more hit-em-high-then-low combination, and it will be in easy reach.

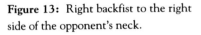

Figure 13: Right backfist to the right side of the opponent's neck.

Figure 14: Dropping the left elbow down on top of the opponent's right forearm—folding his elbow.

Figure 15: Shown from the back.

From the right elbow strike above, the defender delivers a right backfist to the right side of his opponent's neck (fig. 13). Then, using his left elbow, the defender drops his weight and drives his elbow down onto his opponent's right forearm—again near his elbow (fig. 14). (Figure 15 shows the elbow action from the other side.) This does the trick. With the attacker's head now well within range, the defender finishes slamming a right horizontal elbow into his opponent's head (fig. 16).

Using the clear-and-punch concept, the student can clear or check a variety of punch attacks. This alone makes the concept very beneficial. But, armed with an understanding of just one underlying principle, the martial artist now has many more ways in which he can apply the same movement.

An Ancient Chinese Proverb

There is an old Chinese proverb that applies to this concept like no other; it goes like this: "Give a man a fish and you feed him for a day. Teach a man to fish and you feed him for a lifetime." This proverb is about principles. Look for principles and you will discover many concepts. Learn the principles and you will move well beyond technique. Observe, discover, and understand them thoroughly, and you will create your own techniques, spontaneously and dynamically, as the need arises. Then you will be well on your way to becoming an accomplished artist.

Figure 16: Right horizontal elbow into opponent's head.

NOTES

1. Sempok and depok are both ground-sitting positions, but in sempok you step with the traveling leg crossing behind the support leg into the cross-legged ground-sitting position. With depok, the traveling leg crosses in front of the support leg as you step into the position. Sempok and depok are executed with the traveling leg advancing or retreating.

2. In a classic scene from the 1989 Paramount picture *Raiders of the Lost Ark,* the central character, Indiana Jones, faces an Arab who displays deadly skill with his large scimitar. Instead of using his whip or some other impressive weapon, Jones simply pulls out his pistol and shoots his opponent. It is this kind of pragmatic realism that the Western-thinking Dutch bring to Asian martial arts.

3. For those unaware, forms (also called patterns or kata) are roughly equivalent to choreographed shadowboxing.

4. I refer to my instructor's "earlier students" because, since my study with him started in 1983, I fall into the group of Willem de Thouars' "latter students." (The differences in the instruction received by both groups will be addressed later.)

5. Prearranged sets of single techniques called *djurus* (*jurus*) are taught by many instructors of Indonesian arts. However, my instructor, because of his training in Chinese kuntao, taught most of his techniques through his forms.

6. Lucius Annaeus Seneca, c. 3 B.C.–A.D. c. 65

7. Within the martial art community there are practitioners who, when describing their training programs and methods of instruction, routinely use the term "concepts." These individuals are primarily martial artists who study multiple arts and focus on the broader, general ideas or "concepts" of those arts—as opposed to details and other technical specifics.

Chapter 1

From Osmosis to Order

Thumb through any of a number of martial art publications and you will find countless advertisements offering to share the "secrets" for developing speed, power, timing, and other attributes of a winning fighter. Whether we believe these advertisements or not, it would be nice to know how the advertisers' "secret" training methods were developed. Who tested them and how? Likewise, for you to appreciate the training methods detailed in this book, you need to know how they were developed. To see how they were developed, you first need to know something about the normal learning process.

This chapter starts with an explanation of the learning and training method development processes. You are then introduced to four basic methods of entry—

initial responses to punching attacks—that are fundamental to those used consistently by Dutch-Indonesian fighters. You will see these basic methods of entry used throughout the remaining chapters. But first, the learning process.

LEARNING—A THREE-STEP PROCESS

Learning is a very complicated activity, and much has been written about it; however, for our purposes, a simple learning model will suffice. In martial art study, learning results as the student engages in the following three separate but interdependent activities:

- conditioning
- repetition
- observation

This learning progression is continuous and cyclical. It is continuous because the student does not cease working on one level before he moves on to another. It is cyclical because reaching the third (observation) level is not the end. Completion of one cycle only signals the beginning of another round of conditioning, repetition, and observation. The new cycle may or may not mean increased intensity, like harder conditioning; however, it always means that the learning is better focused and the process refined. Although these three stages in the learning process are interdependent, their ascent always begins with conditioning.

Conditioning

Martial artists accept the fact that continuous physical training is an integral part of martial art study. Just as fire cannot continue without oxygen, martial skills cannot remain sharp without physical training and practice. For that reason, the first step in learning martial art skills is conditioning—physical and mental.

Conditioning prepares the mind and body for the physical tasks at hand. Muscles must be strengthened and stretched; neural paths must be established to develop the desired reflexes. Mental conditioning and toughening are also part of the process. One learns, for example, to both expect and accept pain as a part of training;[1] this is true in any athletic endeavor. We must not, however, assume that learning results from this physical activity. Conditioning provides only the physical and mental platform from which learning begins.

Repetition

After initial conditioning, the student can begin drilling. We affectionately refer to this as "practice, practice, practice." This learning by repetition is the basic driver behind the neurological and mental learning that are often called muscle memory.

Popular trapping, sensitivity, and flow drills, like the Filipino *hubud*, wing chun's *chi sao*, and tai chi's *push-hands* are methods of training that provide many repetitions of basic movements. Trainers often use strenuous repetitive training as part of their conditioning regimen. Although this makes better use of the student's training time, it also carries with it some risk. Strenuous repetition of martial art movements results in fatigue; that is the purpose of strenuous exercise. However, fatigue eventually results in sloppy technique, and doing many repetitions of sloppy technique results in learning sloppy technique. Consequently, it makes better sense to separate repetitive training and conditioning exercises, or at least remember that repetitive practice is primarily a training tool and not a conditioning one.

Observation

Observation is the most important and the least understood of the three steps of learning. Martial artists are notorious for overdoing the physical and underdoing the mental (visual) aspects of training. The typical practitioner fails to see the value of just standing back and watching. Nevertheless, the fact remains that observation is a better learning tool than either conditioning or drilling. Let's take a closer look at this learning step.

Among behaviorists, biologists, and physical scientists, it is well known that animals learn by watching. In one study, Italian scientists reported that octopuses learn more quickly by observation than by training (Fiorito and Scotto 1992). The experiments consisted of training octopuses with food and rewards to attack either a red or white ball. Once an octopus had mastered the task of attacking the colored ball, another (untrained) octopus was placed in an adjoining tank. The untrained octopus watched as the trained octopus went through its eight-armed paces. The observing octopus neither watched nor participated in the *training*—it only observed the trained octopus *play*.

When the observing octopuses were allowed to attack the balls, those who had watched the trained octopuses charge red balls dove for a red ball; those who witnessed chases of a white ball swarmed after a white ball. The conclusion? "The observers had not only learned the task but had done so *more rapidly* than the trained group" (emphasis added).

The study's interesting conclusions reinforce personal observations regarding my own training and instruction. Since having neck surgery a few years ago, I have found that my learning, comprehension, and understanding of material presented by my instructor have improved tenfold.[2] Since surgery, my full participation in my instructor's rough-and-tumble training sessions has been limited somewhat. At times I have (as some might see it) been relegated to the position of class videographer. But *relegated* is not the word I use. *Promoted* is more like it.

Observing my instructor from behind the camera as he leads the group through a technique or a form (pattern of movement) and watching the other students as they attempt to perform the same movement teaches me volumes. Through the camera's eye, I observe my instructor at a greater distance than the other participants and with detachment and perspective not available to the others. I see him as he demonstrates a movement before the class, as he repeats and reviews the material, and as he works with each student. As he provides one-on-one instruction, I note how he describes and even alters the material to match the individual's strengths, abilities, and comprehension level. Much of my recent exposure to my teacher's instruction comes not from the "expected" and usual physical training methods; nor does it come from unexpected new and unusual training drills. Rather, like the observing octopuses, I am learning increasingly from observation.[3]

Initially, I thought that the improved learning was simply the result of years "spent with the master." Was I finally seeing and grasping his oft-repeated patterns of movement? Doubtless, that is part of it, but simple time and practice do not account for the bulk of recent progress. Looking back, I know now that what took place in my training is actually a logical progression through the normal learning process.

It is an undeniable fact: humans learn by observing. We observe and learn from our parents, our friends, our idols, our teachers, and, yes, even by observing other species. Proper physical conditioning is essential, and neuromuscular coordination through repetitive training is equally important, but learning by observation is the martial artist's best training tool.

This closely parallels the traditional progression of study in Taoist martial arts. There, one moves from the physically demanding hsing-i boxing to the exacting pakua chang, and finally to the fluid grace of tai chi ch'uan. Tai chi maintains and builds upon the physical conditioning developed in hsing-i and the elevated skills realized by constant practice in pakua, while imparting, almost osmotically, a new level of smoothness and sophistication. Aside from push-hands training, tai chi is learned almost exclusively by observation—one simply follows what the master does.

This method of learning by observation comes only after passing through the preceding levels. Following the conditioning and repetition levels, observation is both the easiest and the most difficult method of learning. It is the easiest because it requires the least effort (physical and mental); one just relaxes and absorbs, learning almost osmotically. Certainly, questions are necessary and practice follows, but this observation part of the basic learning process is effortless.

On the other hand, learning by observation is, for some, the most difficult *because* it requires the least effort. This is especially true for those who train particularly hard—that is, physically hammering it out—day in and day out. For these individuals (and I include myself here), sitting and observing at a seminar or training session seems unthinkable. How can we possibly learn without wearing ourselves out?

Curiously, the observing octopuses were not given a red or white ball with which to practice while they were observing; yet, when they were finally exposed to their target—even without practice—they knew exactly what to do. Conditioning and practice had nothing to do with their success.

In reality, practice without sufficient observation often does more harm than good. It invariably leads to the ingraining of mistakes and habits that must be unlearned later—a terrible waste of precious training time.

UNDERSTANDING THE BASIC LEARNING MODEL

The basic learning model consists of conditioning, repetition, and observation. Conditioning is the foundation. Unlike the foundation laid for a building—something usually done only once—this first phase of training is something that the martial artist *must* maintain throughout the learning cycle. Constant conditioning is necessary because the other two phases of learning—repetition and observation—require a solid and well-maintained foundation.

Without the strong body and disciplined mind that conditioning produces, repetitive practice becomes tiresome, and it ends before the desired reflexes are sufficiently burned in. Repetition is critical if the observed skills and principles are ever to become automatic.

Observation opens our eyes to new possibilities and opportunities for improvement—providing, of course, that we maintain our conditioning and practice (repetition) regimen. All elements of the model are necessary if one expects to reach his fullest potential as a martial artist.

Understanding the learning model should help you see where the drills that follow spring from and how they help us learn, really learn, fighting principles. The model should help you understand the importance of observation in the learning process—something too often ignored, hidden by the sweat in our eyes. The role and usefulness of repetitive training become clear when you begin seeing self-defense applications right out of the drills themselves. Very few training methods offer as much immediate applicability to self-defense as do repetitive training drills. Again, every element of the model is required if the student of the arts ever expects to reach his fullest potential.

DEVELOPING TRAINING METHODS

The drills that grew from the challenge to develop training methods that would simplify the learning process and, at the same time, burn into my mind the principles that make these arts so effective did not spring from some consciously ordered or well-thought-out program. More often than not, the practices, training drills, and teaching methodologies evolved following a natural path that moved from unconscious mechanism, through a period of awareness, and finally to planned development.

Mechanism

The development path begins with unconscious *mechanism*. According to the *Random House Dictionary*, mechanism is, by definition, "a habitual manner of acting to achieve an end." Biological mechanism is "an involuntary and consistent response of an organism to a given stimulus." Applied to martial arts, mechanism is *a habitual, involuntary, and consistent response to a given stimulus*. Simply put, I was unconsciously but repeatedly performing specific patterns of movement that, although not expressly taught by my instructor, had nonetheless become part of my sub- and unconscious response to a given stimulus—a punch, a grab, a kick, or whatever.

These patterns of movement were not taught by my instructor because he assumed that the black belt instructors studying with him already knew them. To him, they were basic. They probably were not formally passed on to him either.

In his culture, the student invariably saved his questions for something really worth the pain of the teacher's answer. These basics, then, were learned primarily through observation. One simply stayed with the teacher long enough and, eventually, the knowledge rubbed off.

Awareness

Following sub- and unconscious mechanism is *awareness*. By awareness I mean the conscious realization that a given movement is being used. For myself, that realization usually came from my students. They noticed the new movement because it was being done to them. Observation again, only this time my students were doing the observing.

Following awareness and recognition of the pattern of movement, my students and I worked together to understand the movement's underlying principle. Once we understood it, we developed a drill that would facilitate learning and assimilation.

Indonesian leg maneuvers are an excellent example of this process. Although they will be described in detail later, let me say here that their development as a training method followed the learning pattern exactly.

My students were the first to notice that I was locking their legs and pinning their feet. After realization—becoming aware of this subconscious pattern of movement—we worked together to understand the movement.

I began "seeing" or consciously recognizing those same patterns of movement in my instructor, as if for the first time. Then, and only then, did I develop formal drills that would help us practice and more quickly share these patterns with others.

Spontaneity by Rote

Train with Willem de Thouars long enough and you begin seeing repeating patterns of movement. I saw this first in his methods of entry. Of the various entries de Thouars uses, his two-hand plays stood out first.[4] I call them *block-right* and *block-left*. Although each is performed on either side, I deliberately decided to practice one method on one side and the other method on the opposite side. The reason for doing this is simple: it forces everyone (my students and myself) to practice both movements.

Normally, when learning new skills, each of us develops preferences. Given two blocking methods, we develop a preference for one over another. By forcing ourselves to practice one on one side and a different one on the other, we end up practicing both movements equally. Over time, the practice of one movement—for example, the one practiced on the right side—eventually bleeds over to the other (left) side, ultimately making us comfortable with both.

Classical "inward" and "outward" blocks are taught only for reference and to give us a common vocabulary. For example, any movement that, complemented by the other arm, results in a clapping action of the hands is called "inward." The opposite is "outward." Beyond that, we use terms that indicate the blocking direction, either left or right.

Block-Right

Block-right takes its name from its action and its direction. Its *action* is a block, a deflection, a protective maneuver that positions the fighter and his weapons for follow-up. Its *direction* (to the defender's right) is where the assailant's weapon and energy are directed. It makes little difference which arm the strike is thrown with, left or right, the movement remains the same; the opponent's arm is directed to the defender's right.

Figure 17

Figure 18

When using block-right, the left hand makes the initial interception of the attacking punch (fig. 17). Because our training is predominantly strong-side forward,[5] the left hand's interception point is necessarily closer to the attacker's fist than his elbow.

Immediately following the left-interception, the right hand rises from beneath the left and provides the bulk of the support needed for the block (fig. 18). From a right lead, strong-side-forward position, the right arm attacks the incoming blow further up the arm than does the initial left.

Figure 19: Defender's left hand intercepts attacker's left jab.

Figure 20: Defender's right arm follows and reinforces the left hand's initial interception.

To demonstrate the movement's utility, its ability to deal with incoming right or left punches, Figures 19 and 20 show the basic block-right maneuver against a left punch. As you can see, against a straight punch, it makes no difference whether the attack is a left or right punch.

The object of any blocking method is twofold: protection and position. Protection is exactly that: protecting your face (or whatever your assailant intends to hit). Position relates to follow-up—what you intend to do after the block. Block-right provides both protection and position, but the *extended* version of block-right really highlights the *position* part of the equation. (To increase the visibility of this "extended version," my partner and I will switch positions.)

In the extended version, the left-hand interception is the same as before (fig. 21). The "following" right-hand right motion, however, *extends*—in this case over the opponent's arm and across his chest (fig. 22). Like the first block-right example you saw, the extended version protects, but it also positions itself more aggressively, penetrating deeper into enemy territory. Figure 23 shows one possible follow-up from this extended position.

Figure 21: Initial left-hand intercept of opponent's right punch.

Figure 22: Defender's right arm extends across opponent's chest.

Figure 23: Right hand drives opponent's head into horizontal left elbow strike.

Block-Left

Like block-right, block-left takes its name from its action and its direction; the action is a block, and its direction is to the defender's left. However, unlike block-right, this maneuver begins with the right hand intercepting the incoming blow farther up the opponent's arm (nearer his elbow than his hand). Here, the movement is used against a left lead jab.

The first photograph (fig. 24) shows the placement of the intercepting right hand near the opponent's left elbow. Simultaneously, as the right hand intercepts the opponent's jab, the left hand is brought to a position forward of the defender's face and close to his right shoulder (fig. 25). This places it in good position to cover or strike.

Immediately following the initial right-hand interception of the attacking jab, the left hand (already positioned at the defender's right shoulder) glides over the right, displacing and reinforcing the initial right-hand deflection, as in Figure 26. (Although used in defense against a left jab, block-left is also an excellent defense against a hooking right haymaker attack.)

It must be pointed out here that a left jab from a trained boxer is so quick that the second hand movement (the displacing left-hand follow-up to the initial right-hand interception) will very likely *not* find an arm there to work against. However, that fact does not alter the effectiveness of the movement. Both block-left and block-right are only basic movements designed for beginners. The problem of a quick left jab is adequately dealt with when we get to the strike-left movement.

Like block-right, block-left also has an extended version. (I will demonstrate this with the defender on the right side in the following sequences.)

Figure 24: Defender's right hand intercepts opponent's left jab.

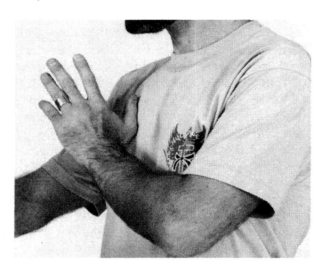

Figure 25: Defender's left hand is positioned high during right-hand intercept.

Figure 26: Defender's left hand displaces his right at opponent's elbow.

Figure 27: Defender's right hand intercepts opponent's left jab.

Figure 28: Defender's left hand clearing opponent's arm.

Figure 29: Defender's left hand extends across opponent's chest.

As in the basic maneuver, the right hand makes the initial interception as the left hand simultaneously moves to its ready position near the right shoulder (fig. 27). From here, the left hand immediately slips over the defender's initial right; however, this time the left extends over the opponent's extended arm and across his chest (or in front of his face), ready to pull back and down (figs. 28 and 29). As with the extended version of block-right, the defender is well positioned for an aggressive follow-up.

Block-right and block-left are, again, basic movements developed for teaching the central principle to beginners. In reality, de Thouars rarely uses these movements in what I call "block mode." As a kuntaoer, he prefers a much more aggressive approach: striking.

Figure 30: Strike-right—intercepts opponent's punch exactly as block-right.

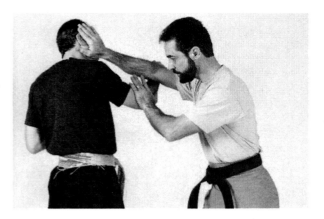

Figure 31: Instead of reinforcing the block, the defender's right hand *strikes* his opponent.

Strike-Right

Like their blocking predecessors, *strike-right* and *strike-left* take their names from their action and direction. By action, their movements are strikes. By dictionary definition, to strike means "to cause to come into violent or forceful contact." Strike-right's action, then, is an aggressive maneuver designed to inflict pain and punish the attacker. Direction indicates both where the action (or strike) takes place and where the opponent will be (relative to the defender's position) during that action; in strike-right, the direction is to the defender's right.

Strike-right, like the blocking maneuver before it, begins with an initial deflection of the incoming right punch by the defender's left hand. As before, the left hand intercepts the attacking blow at or near the opponent's wrist—closer to the attacker's hand than to his elbow (fig. 30). The right hand, *coming from beneath the left*, follows immediately. Only this time it lashes out, striking the opponent on the right side of his face (fig. 31).

Figure 32: Striking with the ulnar side of the wrist.

Figure 33: Using the heavy-hand "wet towel" palm strike.

The second right-hand blow can be an eye poke, a backfist, or any number of other open-hand strikes. (Kuntaoers use a variety of open-hand strikes that land like a weighted rubber hose or a heavy wet towel.) The striking surface may be the ulnar-side (outside) of the defender's right wrist (fig. 32), or it may be a heavy palm strike (fig. 33). With the palm strike, it is important that the defender's striking right hand cover the opponent's eye, obstructing his vision while producing intense pain. (The expression "he never saw it coming" takes on new meaning with this kind of "in-your-face" defense.)

Strike-Left

Strike-left is produced by taking the block-left movement you saw earlier and extending the second (left) hand to strike the head or neck of the attacker (instead of striking or checking his arm). The initial deflection (made by the right hand) is the same as block-left—the defender's right hand picks up the incoming blow on the opponent's forearm, close to his elbow (fig. 34). The "following" left hand (ready at the defender's right shoulder) slides over the defender's right and strikes the attacker's neck, head, or face. As with strike-right, the strike can be made with the hand or palm (fig. 35), the ulnar side of the left wrist (fig. 36), or the fingers (fig. 37).

Figure 34: Defender's right hand intercepts opponent's left jab near the elbow.

Figure 35: Defender's left hand strikes opponent's face.

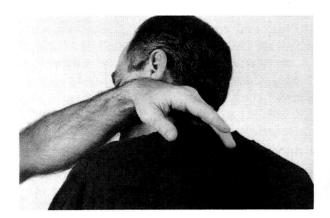

Figure 36: When striking with the ulnar side of the wrist, the hand is very relaxed.

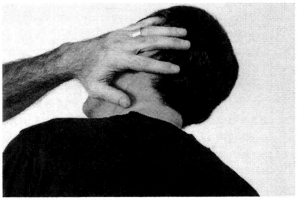

Figure 37: When the hand is relaxed it lands like a heavy wet towel.

Earlier, when describing block-left, I pointed out that against a trained boxer's left jab, the second (follow-up) hand movement—the one displacing the initial right-hand interception of the incoming jab—will likely *not* find the boxer's arm there to work against. I indicated, however, that strike-left works well against a quick jab.

Because strike-left's follow-up left hand strikes the opponent's head, face, or neck instead of continuing to work against his extended arm, it matters little that the opponent's hand or arm is no longer there. As the preceding sequences demonstrate, strike-left's focus is striking, not blocking. As such, the retracted jab is no problem since the attacker's arm is no longer the target; his head is.

Relaxation is the key to mastery of these techniques. In each of these basic blocking and striking scenarios, the hands are relaxed, allowing them to contour to the surface they are striking. They are strong, but they are neither stiff nor rigid. Compare the next two examples.

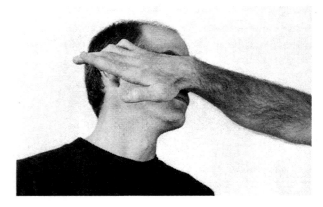 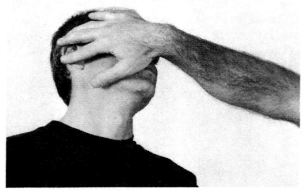

Figure 38: The rigid hand has less surface contact and, therefore, reduced ability to manipulate and control the head.

Figure 39: The relaxed hand has greater surface area contact.

In Figure 38, the hand is tense—strong, but rigid. It is more like a frozen towel than a heavy wet one. The contact surface area is limited with this type of strike. Now, compare it with the next example.

In Figure 39, the hand is relaxed. This allows it to conform to the target surface, thereby increasing the contact area. It is this increase in contact area and the relaxed nature of the hand that makes these "slaps" so painful.

Slapping is used extensively in Indo-Chinese arts. One of the reasons slaps are popular in these arts is because of the almost unbelievable speed with which they are delivered. An open and relaxed hand is many times faster than a strong clenched fist. Even those who hold a low opinion of slapping techniques must agree that the one being slapped is very busy defending himself. That's fine by me, because the longer I can keep my opponent on the defensive, the better my odds are for success.

Slapping often provides the edge that makes the difference between winning and losing. About the only time you would use slapping alone—without following it with some other more destructive tactic—might be at a Friday night party with an obnoxious but relatively harmless drunk. A heavy wet towel might just make him behave, and without having to do any serious damage.

The Best of the Best

These methods of entry, both blocking and striking, are what I consider the "best of the best." Of the four or five "core" entries de Thouars uses, strike-right and strike-left are used 80 percent of the time. Although they appear in some ways more complex than the classical karate blocking methods, they are not complicated—sophisticated yes, complicated no.

Having said that these blocking methods are more sophisticated than "classical karate blocking methods," I must point out that similar methods are practiced on at least the highest level in some classical karate systems. A rare example of this was demonstrated by Sensei Taika Oyata, a ranking authority in Okinawan martial arts, in a recent issue of *Budo Dojo* magazine (Shintaku 1994, 28). There, Sensei Oyata demonstrated two defenses against punching attacks, the first against a left jab and the second against a right cross. In both techniques, he used exactly the block-right blocking method shown in this chapter.

Feeling Is Believing!

Sadly, photographs alone cannot demonstrate the effectiveness of these maneuvers, and one chapter is not enough to explain all their points and subtleties. Only by working with a good Indonesian fighter can you really appreciate these simple but devastatingly effective movements.

In this chapter you learned how the training methods detailed in this book were developed. You saw how their development was tied directly to the normal learning process and specifically from the third, observation phase of that process. Finally, from that basic understanding of the learning and training method development processes, you were shown basic methods of blocking, striking, and entering that sprang directly from their application.

Exploring new things and discovering their underlying principles is a constant process in our school. Because of this, the cement around even these methods of blocking, striking, and entering is likely never to dry. Although they are not the final answer, they do provide methods of training right now that greatly simplify the learning process of these very sophisticated Indo-Chinese arts.

NOTES

1. Accepting pain as a part of training does *not* mean ignoring the pain of injury. Rather, it is the acceptance of the inconsequential and transient pains that are normally associated with overcoming the hardship and discomfort while pursuing one's training goals.
2. Some have suggested that the improvement is because the surgeon really worked on my head, but this suggestion is only the wishful thinking of a few of my closest friends.
3. Do not misunderstand. Neck surgery has neither slowed nor diminished my physical training. I simply avoid the high-risk training exercises that I would have attempted unhesitatingly before. As previously stated, observing my instructor is only my first step to learning what he teaches. Considerable practice *always* follows—much of it is with my teacher's other students, as well as with my own. Observation without practice is *never* enough to make one a proficient martial artist.
4. For me, the term "two-hand" is different from double-hand. A two-hand movement is a sequence of two motions: one, two. Double-hand means both hands at once—simultaneous.
5. Strong-side forward places the fighter's strong hand and foot up front. Orthodox boxing dictates just the opposite and keeps the stronger right hand in reserve.

Chapter 2

Adhesion

In a common combat environment, similar systems of defense develop. Wherever there are commerce, travel, and communication, effective methods of defense will not remain unique. If they are truly effective, they are quickly adopted—and their principles adapted—by others. For example, few will argue that the Japanese brought the art of the sword to its highest level. Even today, study of the Japanese sword, its design and manufacture, and its practice as a martial art remains the passion of millions. However, the introduction of firearms to Japan changed completely and forever the way war would be waged there.

For a time, the firearms imported to Japan were restricted to the ruling elite. However, the effectiveness of firearms could not be denied, and soon everyone was using them. This included samurai who were good with a sword and those who were not. Effective methods of combat will not, cannot, and do not remain unique. Either they are adopted by everyone or they are replaced by even more effective methods. This is a basic law of combat.

One can spend a lifetime studying and mastering a single art or system.[1] Some use this maxim as justification for looking down on those who study more than one. However, it is only by studying and observing several arts that one discovers the many characteristics and principles of movement that even seemingly dissimilar arts have in common.

This ability to recognize commonalities among differing fighting systems and arts is important because it validates the effectiveness of the combat principles taught in the art or system you study. Methods of combat that are truly effective—and their underlying principles—will be found in other fighting arts and systems.

DISTINGUISHING CHARACTERISTICS

Martial artists in the United States have the good fortune to be exposed to martial ways and fighting arts from around the world. This provides us with the exposure and experience we need to identify general characteristics that distinguish one art from another. In our case, we can compare Indonesian arts to others like karate, kung fu, jujutsu, and tae kwon do. But before we can see and understand the differences, we need to begin our study on the same ground by agreeing on a simple and common vocabulary. So armed, we can advance better prepared into the vast and awesome world of Indonesian martial arts.

The arts of the archipelago are so sophisticated that it was more years than I care to admit before I could recognize, describe, and demonstrate (even to my own satisfaction) any characteristics of either pentjak silat or Chinese kuntao. Early in my training, my instructor identified one characteristic for me—he called it *petjut*, or *whiplash*. Although he exposed me to that characteristic early on, it was some time before I understood the principle involved well enough to apply it in a technique. Over time, more characteristics emerged. Four of the more important ones (along with whiplash) are what we call *adhesion, shearing, seating,* and *gyroscopic rotation*. In this and the next few chapters, we'll look at these characteristics with an eye to understanding their underlying principles.

Sticking to Your Opponent

Adhesion is the first and most important principle. Adhesion is the practice of staying so close to your opponent that you appear stuck to him. With adhesion, you use your tactile sense to monitor and control the actions of your opponent. This ability to fight at very close range is a plus for two reasons.

First, the proximity allows the trained fighter to bring more weapons to bear on his foe—weapons like knees, shins, shoulders, and long-, mid-, and short-range elbows.[2] The second reason close-quarter combat distance is a plus is that many confrontations occur at night or in situations where visibility is limited. In those situations, the ability to defend oneself by touch is critical. (Figures 40 through 48 present examples of long-, mid-, and short-range elbow strikes.)

Adhesion as a Fight Strategy

Strategically, adhesion involves the whole body. The following sequence shows how you use this strategy.

Figure 40: Long-range elbow.

Figure 41: Mid-range elbow.

Figure 42: Short-range elbow.

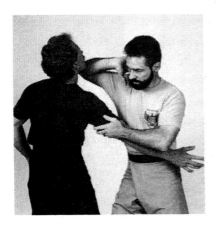

Figure 43: Long-range elbow application.

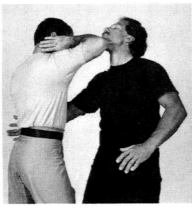

Figure 44: Long-range elbow from the back.

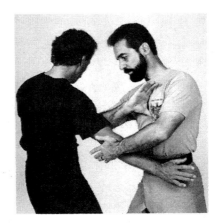

Figure 45: Mid-range elbow application.

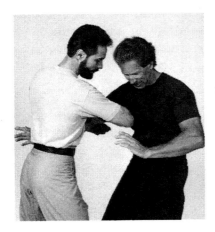

Figure 46: Mid-range elbow application from behind.

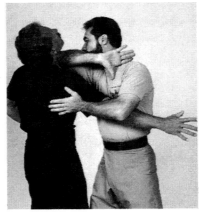

Figure 47: Short-range elbow application.

Figure 48: Short-range elbow application from the back.

Figure 49   Figure 50   Figure 51

In this simplified defense against a left jab, the defender (on the right) slips inside the attacker's punch using a block-right entry (figs. 49 and 50). Shuffling still closer to his opponent, the defender drives a right vertical elbow into the attacker's near ribs while at the same time checking his opponent's right arm (fig. 51). At this point, the defender has elbow, shin, shoulder, and hand contact on the attacker.

Before the attacker can recover from the elbow in his ribs, the defender strikes his face with a right heel-palm (fig. 52). This is both a driving and glancing blow. The driving element is that part that forcefully shoves the assailant's head back. The glancing element follows that and is where recovery and positioning for follow-up take place. It is important to note that only after the attacker's head is shoved back does the blow glance off his face, stopping at a position just past the attacker's face and over his right shoulder (fig. 53). Simultaneous with the strike to the head, the defender's left hand slips up his opponent's right arm to a position near his elbow.

With the defender's right hand positioned at his attacker's right shoulder and his left hand just below his right, the defender grabs his opponent and, pulling, turns him clockwise (fig. 54). Because the defender maintains close contact with his opponent, the clockwise turn twists and traps the attacker's legs. From his badly pretzeled position, the assailant can offer little resistance to a sudden shove from behind (fig. 55). Finishing, the defender follows his man to the ground, keeping the lock on his legs and maintaining a close and strong defensive posture (fig. 56). Notice how the Indonesian fighter remains close enough to his opponent to maintain arm, body, and leg contact throughout the fight.

Although leg control is addressed in depth in the next chapter, it is worth noting now that the purposefully maintained leg-to-leg contact between the combatants is as important to the success of this defense as anything else the defender did in his defense. The tactic of maintaining tight leg contact with the opponent is common among Indonesian fighters, and you will see it used repeatedly in the technical sequences used throughout the remaining chapters.

Figure 52

Figure 53

Figure 54

Figure 55

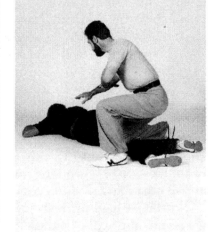

Figure 56

Figure 57: The defender is close enough to cover a weapon if one is discovered.

Figure 58: The defender is too far from his assailant to prevent him from pulling a weapon.

Keeping the attacker close right to the end allows the defender to monitor his attacker's actions, ensuring, for instance, that his opponent is incapable of continuing the fight with some long-range weapon (fig. 57). From this position, if the attacker goes for a weapon, the defender is in a position to stop or check him. That is not true if one's defense knocks the opponent some distance away (fig. 58).

As you can see, adhesion at this level requires continuous contact with the opponent. Loss of contact, or separation from the attacker, gives your opponent an opportunity to escape or counterattack. Sticking to the opponent is critical, and it is something the Indonesian fighters do instinctively.

A *word of caution*: the advisability of prolonged contact or adhesion to an assailant decreases as the number of opponents increases. This is a problem common to grappling arts. In a multiple-attacker situation, staying with any *one* fighter is unwise. While you are taking your assailant all the way to the ground or working with him there, others may jump into the fray. However, in most one-on-one situations, adhesion is an excellent strategy.

So far we have focused on adhesion as the strategic part of a fight. The adhesion principle, however, is also applied tactically.

Tactical Application

Strategically, adhesion means sticking to your opponent with your whole body. Tactical adhesion is maintaining extended (adhesive) contact with an opponent using personal weapons. To see this,

Figure 59   **Figure 60**   **Figure 61**

let's contrast a typical Chinese kenpo technique with an Indonesian variation that uses adhesion.

In Figure 59 , the kenpo fighter has advanced inside his attacker's right haymaker punch and blasted the attacking right arm with an aggressive double-arm initial response. (The double-arm response places the defender's left hand on the attacker's arm between his right elbow and wrist, and the right hand close to his right shoulder, although fig. 59 doesn't show this because the attacker's arm has already been moved away by the attack). Contrary to appearances, this initial move is not a block; it is an all-out attack to the offending arm. Executed aggressively, the move not only stops the attacker's momentum, it also sends him reeling backward.

Following the initial move, the kenpo practitioner can use any number of follow-up combinations, but for this demonstration we will keep it simple. Here the kenpo player shuffles into a horse stance with a right backfist to the attacker's groin, followed immediately by a right backfist to his face (figs. 60 and 61). This outwardly simple technique is really a very effective defense.

Applying the adhesion principle tactically, the Indonesian fighter makes a similar advance inside his opponent's right haymaker attack. However, this time, the defender's right hand is placed on or near the attacker's right biceps with his left hand on his opponent's right forearm. Like the kenpo player, the Indonesian fighter also attacks his opponent's arm, but his approach has a yielding element to it. Not that the defense is less aggressive—far from it. Yielding allows the Indonesian fighter's right forearm to simultaneously smash the opponent's chest, thereby stopping his opponent's charge (fig. 62). Instead of knocking the attacker back, this defense—with the defender's arms and hands absorbing the incoming blow—impales the assailant on the defender's right elbow.

Again, this does not mean that the defense is a passive one. Entry and penetration are every bit as

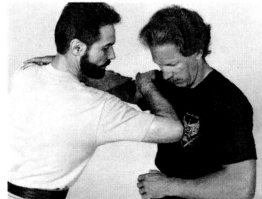

Figure 62

33

Figure 63: Hacksaw strike through the ribs.

Figure 64: Hacksaw strike from the back.

aggressive as the kenpo technique, but the Indonesian objective is to keep the attacker close for follow-up and control.

From the defender's initial interception and punishing counterattack, the defense continues with a unique forearm-strike through the opponent's ribs—one that typifies tactical application of the adhesion principle. Figures 63 and 64 show how the defender's right forearm grinds into his opponent's ribcage.

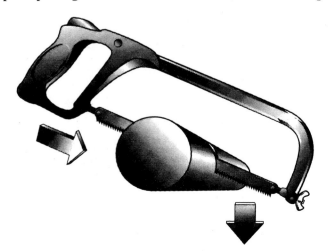

This grind is applied in a hacksaw-like manner. By that I mean that the blow neither chops like an ax nor cuts like a saber. Instead, it saws through the target using a combination of lateral and forward motion. For example, a real hacksaw works not by simply skimming across or gliding over the object it is to cut. It presses into the object as it is pushed along. Equal effort, then, goes into both the downward pressure and the forward motion.

For those still having difficulty seeing this action, here is another example: consider the action of a snowplow. The

blade on a snowplow is mounted at an angle. It has no motion of its own but moves only in the direction of the plow—the vehicle pushing the blade—as it advances through the snow. As the plow moves forward, the blade—locked in its angular position— throws snow off to the side. This is the same action that is used by the hacksaw-forearm. Grasping this point is important if you are to understand the principle of adhesion in general and tactical adhesion in particular.

Returning to our technique, the hacksaw blow through the opponent's ribs softens him up, but, more importantly, it positions the defender to use adhesion again to move his opponent into a position of the defender's choosing. How? The hacksaw's slightly downward angle causes the attacker to fold toward the defender instead of knocking him away.

Bending his elbow, the defender folds his right arm over his opponent's extended arm. This places the defender's right hand near (and a little above) his opponent's elbow (fig. 65). Sticking to his attacker, the defender pivots sharply 90 degrees to his right (clockwise), pulling the attacking right arm through, between himself and his opponent. This violent whipping action turns the antagonist completely around (figs. 66 and 67) while still keeping him close enough to monitor and control. The attacker's vulnerability from this position allows the defender to violently throw him down backward

Figure 65

Figure 66

Figure 67

Figure 68

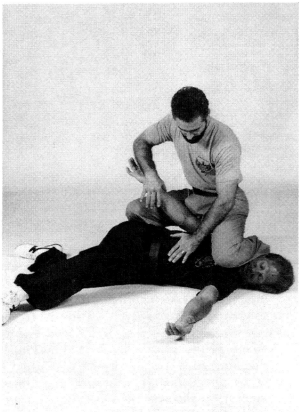

Figure 69

(fig. 68). Finishing the technique, the defender maintains contact with his opponent as he takes him down (fig. 69).

Tactical adhesion is like billiards. When playing billiards, one looks beyond simply sinking a particular ball. Sinking balls is definitely a part of the game; however, for the accomplished player, a more important element of the game is making shots that position the player to make still more. Where the cue ball ends up after the targeted ball is sunk is just as important as the shot itself. This element of position is critical in combat—and one that is lost in many modern martial arts.

The Preeminent Principle

Strategically and tactically, adhesion is very effective. It is presented at the outset for two reasons: first, because the principles and general characteristics that follow all use, require, assume, and build on adhesion. Each principle, by itself, is effective, and each produces amazing results; however, it is when each is combined and used in concert with adhesion that it is most devastating.

The second reason adhesion is described first is because of the psychological hurdle it presents to the martial art student. Although adhesion is a simple principle, it is an intimidating one. Adhesion requires the fighter to move in very close to his opponent and remain there. That is a scary place to be, and very few students coming from other arts ever become comfortable there.

Each of us recoils from pain (real or anticipated): we move out of harm's way. We instinctively turn our faces away from incoming blows. This is a natural reaction. What is unnatural (appearing downright suicidal) is moving in close. However, for the fighter trained in close-quarter combat, staying inside your opponent's normal (comfortable) range is often safer than remaining farther away. Inside, you monitor and control his movements. Outside, you have much less control.

In any fight, you have to position yourself close enough to your opponent to strike him. Except in traditional sport karate matches, very few fights take place at long range where the combatants play "dueling banjos" with their kicks. Despite this reality, very few learn how to fight in close. The popularity of tae kwon do has taught many how to kick (long-range striking). Most, even without training, know how to punch (mid-range). A few know how to grapple, wrestle, or at least roll around in the dirt (close-range). But very few really know how to fight "inside." This is obvious when you consider how few recognize the difference between long-, mid-, and short-range elbow strikes. It makes sense, then, to learn and become comfortable with close-quarter combat.[3] Once you are comfortable with this kind of "infighting," adhesion becomes an excellent fighting tool.

NOTES

1. Here, the terms "art" and "system" are used synonymously. In reality, a martial *art* (e.g., karate, jujutsu, kung fu) is an umbrella that covers or includes many systems and subsystems (e.g., shotokan, isshin-ryu, and goju-ryu are all systems beneath the karate umbrella).

2. I said before that Indonesian fighting arts are very sophisticated; here is an excellent example of that. For most of us, elbows are short-range weapons. End of statement. Indonesian fighters, on the other hand, see them in much greater detail. To them, this close-range weapon has its own long, mid, and short ranges.

3. It is always better to avoid attacking an opponent's strength. If the opponent has good in-fighting skills, then do not fight him there. Use some other—possibly long-range—tactic instead. Beyond that, as a general rule, fighting in close is preferable to fighting from afar.

Chapter 3

Petjut

(Whiplash)

The second general characteristic observable in Indonesian arts is *whiplash*. Most of us have a general understanding of what whiplash is. Certainly, anyone unfortunate enough to suffer neck trauma from a rear-end automobile collision knows firsthand how painful and disabling it can be. Random House defines a whiplash injury as "a neck injury caused by a sudden jerking backward, forward, or both, of the head."

Applied martially, whiplash is *an explosive and violent change in direction used to incapacitate an opponent.* An Indonesian fighter produces this effect by first soliciting a reaction from his opponent and then using that reaction to defeat him.

USING AN OPPONENT'S REACTION AGAINST HIM

Using an opponent's strength against him is not new; many martial arts use this principle. Whiplash, on the other hand, uses an opponent's involuntary and natural reaction and resistance as its principle of destruction. Although this action resembles the whiplash effect that comes from an automobile accident, it is actually more vicious.

As an offensive martial art tactic, whiplash works like this: the initial action, although violent and painful in itself, is designed to elicit a second violent reaction. Unlike the whiplash visualized in the automobile accident (usually a single, one-time reaction to the impact), whiplash as a fighting tactic applies force and reverses it two or more times in rapid succession.

The simplest example of this principle is demonstrated by attempting to pull an individual down from behind. (The antagonist may be assaulting someone else by pinning him against a wall.) Providing the defender is strong enough, he could simply grab the assailant from behind by the shoulders or the scruff of the neck and pull him to the ground. However, this approach brings with it high risk and a low probability of success.

The low probability of success is because pulling an assailant down from behind, especially one who is larger or stronger, is not as easy as it appears. For the aggressor, resistance is easy. Moreover, the antagonist can easily turn on the defender because the defender's approach has not, even momentarily, incapacitated him. Whiplash resolves both of these problems.

Applying the whiplash principle in the scenario just described, the defender first knocks the individual forward, perhaps with a glancing double-palm blow that hits the back of the aggressor's shoulders, skips off, and continues past them. In the split second when the attacker's reaction kicks in

Figure 70: Shoving opponent forward.

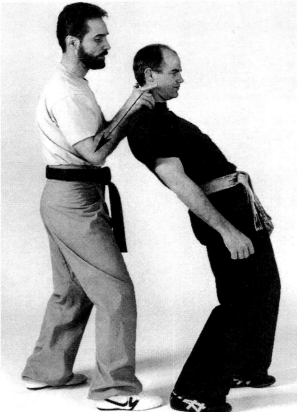

Figure 71: Whipping the opponent back.

Figure 72   Figure 73

and he begins to recover, resisting the initial shove, the defender reverses direction, hooking his hands on his opponent's shoulder and yanking him back (figs. 70 and 71). What makes this tactic so effective is the whip *back*.

The whip capitalizes on the attacker's natural reaction to the initial shove by accelerating his resistance and desire to push back. Any resistance the opponent would have mounted to a simple backward pull is defeated by the defender because he first shoves his opponent forward (eliciting his resistance) and then pulls him backward, capitalizing on his reaction to pull him down. Further, the defender reduces his opponent's ability to turn and counterattack because he is momentarily occupied with an immediate need to regain his balance.

The whiplash principle works equally well when facing an opponent. Once again, the defender begins with both hands striking forward, glancing off the front of the opponent's shoulders and continuing past them (fig. 72). In the split second when the attacker's reaction causes him to resist and he begins to recover from the initial shove, the defender reverses the direction (fig. 73) and whips his opponent forward (toward him). This brings the opponent's head or face crashing into a nasty head-butt.

WHY WHIPLASH WORKS

Whiplash works because it is based on the truth that *one cannot effectively resist force in more than one direction at a time.* Try this simple test. Have your training partner extend his arm toward you, his

Figure 74: Pushing with the arm.

Figure 75: Preparing to slap the arm down.

Figure 76: Right hand exerts downward force.

Figure 77: The one pushing is unable to resist force from more than one direction.

hand formed in a fist. Place his fist in your hand and have him push forward with a steady, even force. As he pushes, resist enough to hold him in place. Then slap his arm with your other hand (figs. 74 and 75). Slap it left, right, or down (the direction is unimportant right now). As shown in Figures 76 and 77, your partner will be unable to maintain his forward pressure and simultaneously resist your slap (which is coming from a direction different from his line of force). This is the secret of whiplash's effectiveness. (You will see more examples of this principle in the sections that follow.)

WHIPLASH IN ACTION

The preceding examples are simple, but they accurately show the whiplash principle. Here now are a couple of techniques that will give you some idea of the principle's utility.

In this defense against a left-grab/right-punch combination, the defender uses the whiplash principle on a horizontal plane (rather than the vertical plane shown before). The attacker begins by grabbing the defender's chest or lapel with his left hand and chambering his right fist to punch. Here is the defense. First, a quick but painful heavy-handed left-hand slap to the opponent's neck and face disrupts his timing and simultaneously positions the defender's left hand to pick up the incoming right punch that is expected to follow (fig. 78). Although the photo doesn't show this, the defender also slaps his opponent's grabbing left hand. This produces no real pain, but it does provide two other benefits: it confuses and distracts the attacker, and it positions the defender's right hand above his

Figure 78

Figure 79: Hacksaw clear and head pull.

43

assailant's left. (This gives the appearance of a possible counterstrike.) However, a right counterpunch is not the intent, for it is really not as practical as it might appear. For example, a stiffened left arm from the attacker can easily stop a right counterpunch. Instead of a right punch here, the defender uses his right hand to cast off the left-hand grab.

In Figure 79, the defender clears his attacker's grasping hand by hacksawing his own right forearm down the inside of the grabbing left arm. He does this by aiming his fingers toward his opponent's left hip (not to strike with, but to set his arm's direction). Simultaneously, as the defender drives his assailant's left arm down, he uses his left hand to hook the assailant's neck and pull him in. This left-hand pull, in concert with the right-hand clearing action, pulls the assailant into the proverbial web. (It often pulls his face violently into a butt with the defender's right shoulder.) Now for the application of whiplash.

Immediately after clearing the opponent's grab and pulling him in, the defender's right palm strikes his opponent's left shoulder with a glancing blow that knocks his shoulder away. Simultaneously, the defender's left hand slaps the back of his opponent's right shoulder, as in Figure 80. (In this action, the defender advances on his assailant as he executes this double-strike maneuver.) The simultaneous right-push and left-pull start the opponent rotating counterclockwise—the first half of the whip.

In the fraction of a second when the assailant begins resisting the counterclockwise rotation, both of the defender's hands reverse direction. Only this time his right hand, like a windshield wiper,

Figure 80   Figure 81

Figure 82

Figure 83: Shearing horizontal elbow strikes pretzeled opponent.

returns, striking the opponent's face as the left hand simultaneously strikes the back of his head, as in Figure 81. The left and right hands, working in concert, begin an opposite, clockwise head rotation that produces a violent and rapid change in direction. This is whiplash at its best. (Although these are glancing blows, they are, nevertheless, very painful to both face and neck.)

Figure 82 presents the ending position of Figure 81's action. The defender's left arm—across his opponent's shoulder blades—prevents the antagonist from spinning out (clockwise) of his entangled and twisted position. The defender's right arm is also now chambered for its next move. Finally, as the assailant strains to save his neck (trying to turn his head back), he meets an onrushing right horizontal elbow smash to his face (fig. 83).

Figure 84: From the grip.

Figure 85: Pulling the opponent right.

Figure 86: Whipping opponent left.

This use of whiplash is common in Indonesian arts; however, its principle is used in other arts as well. Consider the following kenpo technique. Here, the attacker feigns an offer to end a confrontation by presenting his right hand in a mock gesture of peace (fig. 84). However, peace is not his desire—surprise attack is. The antagonist's supposedly peaceful display is a prelude to a surprise left punch or an attack from another avenue—perhaps from one of his buddies. No matter, with whiplash the defender can easily thwart his plan.

Slapping the back of his opponent's grasping right hand and clasping it firmly between his hands (fig. 85), the defender uses an explosive move to pull his opponent forward (toward him) and off to his right. Before his antagonist can recover (attempting to regain his balance—a natural reaction), the defender whips his opponent's arm back (fig. 86). As he does, he lifts the arm up (fig. 87), steps

Figure 87: Lifting opponent's arm.

Figure 88: Stepping through.

Figure 89: Pulling down from behind.

46

under it (fig. 88), and violently pulls it down behind his surprised opponent (fig. 89). This is effectively a double whip.

From this position, the assailant can mount only minimal resistance and is therefore easily controlled—or used as a human shield (possibly between the defender and his opponent's companions). In either case, whiplash plays a large part in this defense.

This example from kenpo is not unique. Many systems incorporate the whiplash principle. One need only be made aware of it to recognize its use within other arts and systems. What makes whiplash unique in Indonesian fighting arts is the fact that the silat fighter or kuntaoer is very much aware of its capabilities and employs it fully as a major weapon in his arsenal.

The application of the whiplash principle is a classic example of using an opponent's strength (or in our case, his natural reaction and resistance) against him. It works because of the timeless truth that one can effectively resist (or exert) force only in one direction at a time. Rapid and frequent changes in direction are the hallmarks of whiplash. As you can see, this principle is aptly named, for it is as vicious as its name implies.

Chapter 4

Gyroscopic Rotation

Like whiplash, gyroscopic rotation capitalizes on the fact that one cannot effectively resist force in more than one direction at a time. However, unlike whiplash, which uses linear motion, gyroscopic rotation is circular. Whiplash is linear because it starts motion in one direction and then reverses that direction (180 degrees) as the opponent resists the initial action. Gyroscopic rotation is circular and takes its name from the gyroscope-like changes in direction it uses. What do I mean by "gyroscope-like changes"? Without getting too technical, the *Concise Columbia Encyclopedia* (1983) defines a gyroscope as follows:

> A symmetrical mass, usually a wheel, mounted so that it can spin about an axis in any direction. *A spinning gyroscope will resist changes in the orientation of its spin axis* [emphasis added].

49

An example of a gyroscope's resistance to changes in axle orientation can be demonstrated using a simple bicycle wheel. Hold a bicycle wheel by the axle's ends. Keep it in front of you with your arms extended. Have someone spin the wheel rapidly and you have a crude but functional gyroscope. Turn to one side or the other and the gyroscope's resistance to changes in the orientation of its axis causes the wheel to turn on its side (turning against its axis). Figures 90 and 91 show this.

Gyroscope.

As a martial art tactic, this gyroscopic action begins by first starting a rotation about an axis. As resistance to the rotation is met, the direction is changed. However, the change in direction is not a reversal as it is in whiplash. Rather, the change in direction is against the axis itself. Visualizing a schoolroom globe will help here.

Imagine your left palm (your thumb pointing down) on the equator of a globe. Rotate the globe counterclockwise. At some point in the rotation, imagine suddenly pulling back against the globe's

Figure 90: Holding a spinning bicycle wheel.

Figure 91: Turning left with the wheel tilts it horizontal.

axis. Now, imagine doing the same thing to a man's head and neck, where his head is the globe and his neck is the axis. As you might imagine, this tactic is as devastating as it is painful.

EXAMPLES OF GYROSCOPIC ROTATION

Gyroscopic rotation is executed from either a left or right lead (with the left or right foot forward) and with either hand. However, to maintain continuity with the globe example, we will use the principle in a technique that administers the movement with the left hand. Also, although the attack that is defended against is not as common in the United States, for better visibility, we will use a right punch from a right lead (in the United States, a punching attack is more commonly initiated using a right punch from a left lead).

As the assailant throws a right punch, the defender slips outside of it using the strike-right multihand combination (fig. 92). Remember, in strike-right, your left hand, as in a classical inward block, makes a quick inward deflection (from left to right) of the incoming punch. Immediately, your right hand follows, coming from beneath and inside your left, striking your opponent's face (fig. 93).

Figure 92: Strike-right initial deflection . . .

Figure 93: . . . and strike to the face.

Although this open-hand strike is very relaxed, it is not at all light or airy. Remember, it lands like a heavy wet towel or a rubber hose.

Following the initial deflection and strike, the defender advances, stepping through with his left

Figure 94: Left forearm strikes the neck.

Figure 95: Begin counterclockwise rotation . . .

Figure 96: . . . then pull back against the axis.

foot and driving his left forearm into his opponent's neck or face. Simultaneously, he pulls his attacker's extended right arm across his chest (fig. 94). His left hand then clings to his opponent's face and begins turning it away from him with a counterclockwise rotation (fig. 95).

As his assailant resists the rotation (fighting his way back), the defender changes the direction of the movement (fig. 96). Only instead of simply reversing the force, as we would with whiplash, the new direction is against the attacker's rotational axis (his neck). Notice that in this technique the gyroscopic rotation is accomplished with only one hand: the left hand starts the rotation *and* completes the neck-breaking action.

Although gyroscopic rotation is the main contributor to the technique's success, other elements contribute to its effectiveness. For example, covering the attacker's eyes as you rotate his head causes disorientation. Attacking his eyes (putting your fingers in them) might increase the technique's brutality, but it also introduces another reaction the defender has to control. For that reason, we limit the response (the defense) to primarily head and neck manipulation.

Look, Ma! Two Hands!

In this next defense against a right punch, *both* hands are used to effect the gyroscopic action. As before, the defender slips outside his assailant's punch using the block-right multihand combination you should be familiar with by now (fig. 97).

As the defender shuffles forward, closing the distance between himself and his attacker, his right palm (his fingers pointed to the right) strikes the right side of his attacker's face (fig. 98). With his hand sticking to his opponent's face, the defender begins a counterclockwise rotation of his opponent's head (fig. 99).

Before the assailant can recover (just as he begins to resist the rotation), the defender's left hand reaches over his right and pulls his opponent's head backward, as in Figure 100 (breaking the axis). Finishing, the defender seats or drops into a horse stance, smashing his foe on to the anvil formed by his knee (fig. 101).

Figure 97: Begin with block-right.

Figure 98: Defender's right palm strikes opponent's face.

Figure 99: Begin rotation.

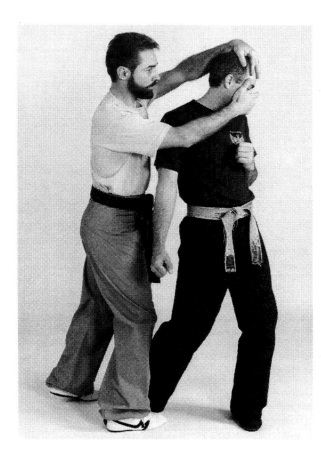

Figure 100: Rotation applied with two hands.

Figure 101: Attacker impaled on defender's right knee.

DEVASTATING—AND DANGEROUS

Gyroscopic rotation is one of the most devastating principles found in Indonesian martial arts; *it is also the most dangerous to practice*. The trauma and pain to the neck can be so severe that even practicing this principle under supervised and controlled conditions is risky. Consider the following.

One of my training partners, an excellent martial artist with a large, well-established school, reported a period when several of his students suddenly began complaining of severe headaches. After conversations with each of them, my friend determined that the headaches may have been the result of practicing these Indonesian techniques involving gyroscopic rotation.

To test his theory, he halted its practice for one month. To everyone's pleasant surprise, the headaches ceased. After a month, practice was resumed, and within a short period the headaches returned. Since then, practice of these very dangerous techniques is kept at a safer level. The experience of this veteran instructor is a warning for us all. These principles *are* dangerous, and even practicing them is something we must do with great care.

Chapter 5

Shearing

Enhancing Effectiveness

S hearing is the application of opposing forces along parallel lines. Its value to the martial artist lies in its ability to enhance the effectiveness of other movements and techniques. In one respect, shearing is like hip rotation: by itself, it's not very impressive. However, marry it to a weapon and it has the same impact as adding oxygen to hydrogen— it makes the weapon highly explosive. Let's understand this quality by examining the dynamics of an elbow strike and see how the shearing principle enhances it.

Elbows are clearly the martial artist's most devastating weapons. As such, anyone unfortunate enough to be on the receiving end of an elbow strike can expect to be knocked away by the force of the blow. Unfortunately, allowing an opponent to fall away from any blow reduces the energy he receives from it. Because of this, elbow strikes should always be executed with a complementing hand.

Figure 102: Classical elbow strike.

Figure 103: Elbow strike using the pincer complement.

Figure 104: Using the shearing principle.

The series of photos shows a horizontal elbow strike with the complementing hand in the *classical* position (fig. 102), the *pincer* position (fig. 103), and the less-recognized *shearing* position (fig. 104). Of the three positions, the second one—where the complementing hand plays directly opposite the elbow strike—is the most popular. Let's begin with that one.

PINCER ACTION

The complementing "pincer" hand uses an action that, like the jaws of pincers, brings two opposing forces crashing together at a single point. Effectively, the complementing hand provides a stop for the target (much like an anvil does for the tool being forged by the hammer). Without the complementing pincer (as in the classical position), the target receives only a fraction of the energy directed toward it. This is especially important when we use this high-powered weapon against a low-mass target, like the head.

The pincer action of the complementing hand reduces the energy loss by keeping the target in place, thereby forcing it to absorb more of the energy of the blow. The pincer action, however, only *reduces* the energy loss. It does not eliminate it because the complementing hand itself absorbs part of the force of the blow. Nevertheless, this pincer-action principle is dramatically more effective than a similar blow without the complementing arm.

SHEARS VERSUS PINCERS

As its name implies, shearing is less like the pincer action of tongs or pliers and more like scissors and shears. Like the pincer action, shearing uses opposing lines of force. However, unlike the pincer, the lines of force never meet or converge at a single point, as shown in the illustration.

Using a horizontal elbow strike similar to the one before, we have the complementing left hand working again in concert with the right elbow strike. This time, however, the hand is on a

separate but parallel plane. As the striking right elbow drives the opponent's head back, it meets an opposing edge—created by the position of the complementing left hand. As the head is driven back, the opponent's neck is sheared between these two opposing forces. (Figures 105 through 107 show the complementing hand's position when used in classical, pincer, and shearing applications.)

You may wonder, if the head is moving away on impact, aren't we back to our original energy-loss problem? The answer is no.

Using the shearing principle, the left complementing hand does not simply hold the opponent in place. In application, it drives the opponent (the target) into the oncoming elbow (the weapon) causing a "head-on" collision. Admittedly, in this example, the complementing hand does not drive the assailant into the weapon with any great speed because it is trying to move the assailant's body, but as you will see, the principle significantly accelerates targets of lesser mass. Moreover, in this technique, any loss in trauma to the impact area is more than offset by the additional (collateral) damage caused to the attacker's neck.

There are other self-defense benefits to shearing as well. For example, with shearing the attacker is effectively clotheslined—dropped where he stands. Having been taken off his feet by the shearing action, the assailant is unceremoniously dumped at the defender's feet. This allows the defender to monitor and control his opponent until safety is assured.

Figure 105: Classical application: least effective. The target is allowed to yield to the force of the blow.

Figure 106: Pincer application: significantly more energy is transmitted to the target.

Figure 107: Shearing application: yielding from the blow results in collateral (neck) damage.

SCISSOR HANDS

Let's look now at the shearing principle in a technique that uses the hands as well as the elbows. In this defense against a straight right punch, the defender slips outside the attacker's punch and advances with an extended block-right combination (fig. 108). (This is the same one-two, left-inward/right-outward combination you should be familiar with by now, only this time the defender's right arm is extended across his opponent's chest, trapping the attacker's right arm below the defender's right-arm block.)

Like a windshield wiper, the defender's right palm returns, striking his opponent's face. Simultaneously, the defender's left palm slaps the back of his opponent's shoulder, driving it in the opposite direction (fig. 109). Like the shearing elbow strike you saw before, this shear uses opposing force on separate planes, only this time the hands act as the shearing weapons. Timing the strike to the face so that it is simultaneous with the blow to the back of the attacker's shoulder forces the head to rotate well past normal range. This results in cervical disc, vertebrae, or ligament damage. In application, if everything works, the defense would probably stop here (not many could continue hostilities after that); however, I said that this technique would use both shearing hands and elbows, so let's continue.

From the right palm strike to the attacker's face, the defender's right hand returns (inside his

Figure 108: Extended block-right.

Figure 109: Left hand pushes opponent's near shoulder forward as defender's right hand strikes the far side of assailant's face back.

Figure 110: Right hammer wrist strikes opponent's ribs.

Figure 111: Hammer wrist as seen from the back.

Figure 112: Elbow strike using the shearing principle.

Figure 113: Shearing shown from the back.

left) and arcs down to a right hammer-wrist strike to the ribs or kidney, as in Figure 110. (The reason the defender's right hand returns inside his left is that his left hand is busy maintaining pressure on the attacker's right shoulder). A hammer fist may be substituted for the hammer wrist if desired, but the wrist is especially suited to this target area. (Fig. 111 shows the hammer-wrist strike from the back side.) Now for the final shear.

Following the right hammer-wrist strike, the defender shuffles still closer to his opponent, driving a shearing horizontal right elbow smash into his face (fig. 112). As you can see, the shear is accomplished using the right elbow in concert with the left hand (fig. 113). (Please note that in actual application the defender would be much closer to his opponent than what is pictured here.)

Figure 114: Strike-left inside a right haymaker punch.

Figure 115: Shearing opponent's biceps.

EXTREMITY DESTRUCTION

In this technique we have another double application of the shearing principle. This time, the defender begins by moving inside his opponent's right haymaker attack with a strike-left combination (fig. 114). Assuming the attacker's right arm is where the defender can still reach it, the defender's left hand (which is already in the attacker's face) slips down the assailant's arm to approximately his elbow. There, the defender pulls his opponent's right arm into a rising right vertical-elbow strike (fig. 115). Often referred to as "biceps destruction," this shearing action drives the tip of the defender's elbow into his opponent's humerus or arm bone. It bears repeating that the shear is accomplished with the left hand *simultaneously* thrusting the attacker's right arm toward the defender's elbow strike. This maneuver often paralyzes and immobilizes the assailant's arm.

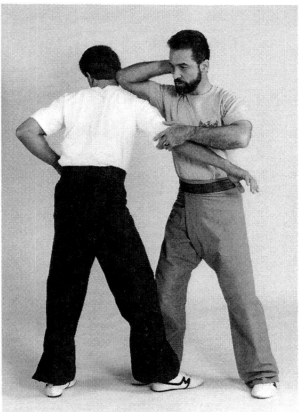

Figure 116: Outside wing-elbow strike to opponent's face turns his head.

Figure 117: Defender's right hand strikes opponent's groin in shear-like action.

As the attacker's arm drops away, the defender fires off a quick right outward *wing-elbow* to his opponent's head or face (fig. 116). This starts a motion that concludes with the defender's right hand circling down and around to strike his assailant's groin. Simultaneous with the groin strike, the defender's left hand slaps the opponent's shoulder from behind, pulling him forward (fig. 117).

Although technically not a true shear, this shear-like action has many of the same characteristics. The slap to the attacker's shoulder is one half of the motion; the other half is the groin strike. The two together produce a shear-like action. The difference this time is that the shear is applied along opposing arcs (sides of a circle), much like the forces pictured in the yin/yang symbol. The technique is, nevertheless, a good example of the shearing principle in both close and mid ranges.

Many kenpo players will recognize this type of palm strike to the groin. Likewise, Filipino martial artists are well versed in extremity (biceps) destruction. All of which reinforces the truth that if a fighting principle of movement is effective, that principle will be found in other effective systems of defense. Here, now, is a long-range example.

At Long Range

In this example, the defender is on the ground. He may have consciously dropped to this position, as harimau[1] practitioners often do, or simply found himself there in the course of the fight. In any case, shearing can quickly turn this seemingly inferior position to one of advantage.

Figure 118: Fighting from the ground.

Figure 119: Right heel strikes inside of opponent's left knee.

Figure 120: Close-up of shearing action.

In Figure 118, the defender's legs are held slightly apart like a pair of open shears, poised to deliver a barrage of brutal strikes. The defender's right leg is positioned in the foreground and above his left. Closing his legs around his attacker's lead left leg[2] as in Figure 119, the defender cuts sharply through his assailant's support (fig. 120). This example of long-range shearing should, at the very least, drive the attacker to the ground. Executed with intent, this long-range shear produces broken bones or permanent knee and ligament damage.

Because of its versatility, shearing is used extensively in Indonesian arts. As you can see, this principle is used to strike a variety of targets (extremities, the head, and body) with a number of personal weapons (elbows, hands, and feet). On the versatility scale alone, shearing ranks high because of its utility. Add to that its ability to significantly enhance the effectiveness of the fighter's techniques, and you can see that shearing is perhaps the least heralded and most underrated of fighting principles.

NOTES

1. The Indonesian system of harimau (ha-REE-mau) specializes in ground-level combat that literally cuts an upright opponent's legs out from under him.
2. Harimau practitioners frequently drop from an upright position to one that traps their opponent's legs.

Chapter 6

Seating

Another principle that is used extensively in Indonesian fighting arts is seating. Seating is a sudden and explosive drop in the fighter's vertical position, as in dropping from a standing position to a crouch. Seating serves many functions, but the primary one relates to a characteristic discussed earlier: adhesion.

Seating allows the fighter to stick with his opponent all the way to the ground. Among silat and kuntao practitioners, seating is most often applied from a squatting horse. The choice of the horse stance for seating is not a matter of casual preference. The relationship between this classical fighting stance and seating is so significant that one cannot fully appreciate the effectiveness of the seating principle without a thorough understanding of the classical horse.

Indonesian martial artists often refer to their tactics as belonging to either the upper art (focusing primarily on hand and elbow skills) or lower art (striking and utilizing the legs). Thus far, we have concentrated on upper-art principles: adhesion, whiplash, gyroscopic rotation, and shearing. With our examination of seating, we move into the realm of the lower art.

THE CLASSICAL HORSE STANCE AND VERTICAL STRENGTH

From an engineering perspective, the horse stance is an excellent example of strength and stability. Its wide base creates a triangular design that enables the fighter to resist tremendous lateral pressure (fig. 121). Its obvious weakness is its instability from the front and back (fig. 122). Despite this, across Asian martial arts, no stance is more highly regarded and valued than the fighting horse.

There is, however, another line of strength that this classical stance offers, and it is one that few recognize: vertical strength. The usefulness of this attribute is beneficial from both training and self-defense (application) perspectives. Let's begin with the training benefit and move to the benefits offered in self-defense.

The Horse in Training

Our practice is reflected in our performance. To the martial artist, this means that what we do in training we will do in application. This does, however, present some problems. How, for example, do

Figure 121: The strength of the horse is its ability to resist lateral force.

Figure 122: The weakness of the horse is from the front and back.

Slapping the mat.

we practice crippling and potentially lethal techniques without injuring our training partners? We begin by accepting the fact that there are things we do in training that we would not attempt in the street. We also recognize that the habits we acquire in training have the potential to be as dangerous as the perils we train to avoid. An example is slapping the mat.

When you work on a mat and you are taken down, slapping the mat protects you from injury. Soft surfaces (and the training practices and habits acquired to work on those surfaces) are necessary if the student is ever to become proficient with techniques that take the fighter down. However, slapping the mat was never intended for use in today's urban environment (try slapping asphalt or concrete). Since there is no acceptable training replacement for this practice, we are forced to accept its streetwise risks in lieu of its training benefits. However, there is another training habit that is much, much less acceptable, and one that the vertical-strength attribute of the horse stance easily resolves: bending over. The habit of bending over to help your training partner gently land on the floor poses great risk for both players. I use the word "habit" here because, except for specific throwing techniques taught in judo and jujutsu, I know of no art in which bending over an opponent is part of the formal instruction. (Usually, bending over is picked up by those with little takedown or throwing experience.)

Helping your partner by bending over him, although understandable, is inherently dangerous. Because bending over to help someone is so natural, it quickly becomes an acquired habit. Moreover, bending over is one habit that is (unconsciously) reinforced by still other training practices, for example, bending over an individual to strike him with an elbow.

Even among those who routinely practice elbow strikes, the habit of bending over an opponent

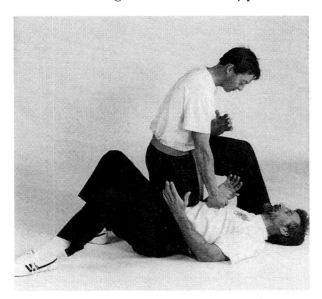

Figure 123: Punching a downed opponent allows the defender to remain erect.

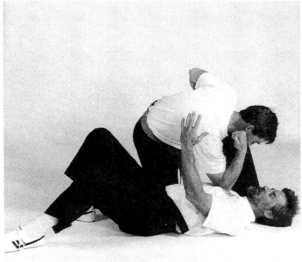

Figure 124: Elbowing a downed opponent is dangerous.

and striking him with the elbow is observed far too often. The student doing this may be standing or already kneeling down. However, instead of executing a kick, knee, or punch on his downed opponent, the student decides to bend over his make-believe foe and finish his technique with a downward elbow smash (compare figs. 123 and 124). This may look "cool," but it is a poor practice and one that negatively reinforces the bending-over habit.

The problem with bending over your opponent is that it places your head within easy reach where it can be seized or hit. As far as helping your training partner, bending over him is actually more dangerous than helpful—for both of you. Bending over is dangerous for the one going down, because the one standing may not be strong enough to hold him and ease him down. It is also hazardous to the one standing for the same reason: bending over someone while attempting to hold him up places the back in the worst possible position, and back injury becomes a real concern. There is, however, a simple solution: seating.

Unlike bending over, which uses back strength, seating uses leg strength (compare figs. 125 and 126). Seating, with the back held erect, accomplishes two important things: first, the one standing is better able to support the weight of his partner because the legs (the major muscle groups used in seating) are much stronger than the back. Second, the head and body are not "hung out" over the opponent—within easy reach, as in Figure 127.

In seating, the triangular geometry of the horse stance (with its vertical-strength attribute) strengthens the defender's position. This allows him to direct his opponent's motion (or control his training partner's) without bending over. Holding the high ground, the defender towers over his foe. At his feet, his assailant is in the inferior position. (This does not mean that he is helpless, but it does—if he knows enough to use it—give the defender a strong advantage.) In training, seating enables even a smaller individual to help his partner down, and with less risk of injury for both.

In the training environment, the vertical-strength attribute of the horse protects the martial artist by enforcing safer training. Let's look now at how the horse, and specifically its vertical-strength attribute, is used as a combat weapon in seating.

Figure 125: Bending over your partner is risky for both of you.

Figure 126: The squatting horse makes it easier to hold up your partner.

Figure 127: Bending over an opponent places the defender's head within easy reach.

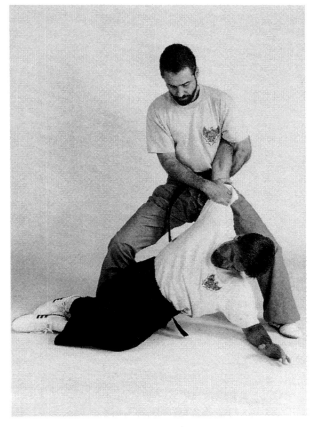

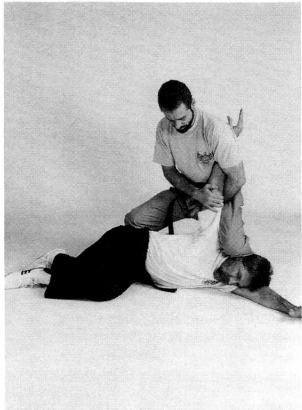

Figure 128: Holding a man up by his arm using a standing horse.

Figure 129: Pressing down on the opponent with the squatting horse.

The Horse in Combat

Again, seating is a sudden and explosive drop in the fighter's vertical position. Seating is effected primarily from one of two horse stances: the *standing* horse and the *squatting* horse. The difference between these two stances is simple: the standing horse exerts force *upward* (fig. 128), as when resisting an opponent's attempt to pull you down. A squatting horse, on the other hand, presses *down* (fig. 129), resisting upward pressure (for example, an opponent at your feet who is attempting to recover to an upright position). With these two horse stances, seating is executed in the following ways:

1. actively—bringing your weapon to the target
2. passively—bringing your target to the weapon
3. indirectly
4. evasively

Active Seating

Active seating is where the defender's knees and shins attack his already "downed" opponent. It uses primarily a squatting horse stance and has the defender actively striking his opponent with the seating action itself. For example, after taking his opponent down, the defender follows him, pressing

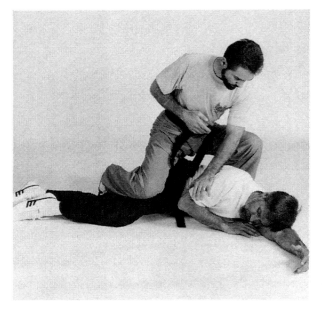

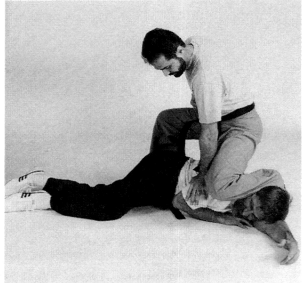

Figure 130: Pressing with his right knee, the defender prevents his opponent from counterattacking with his legs.

Figure 131: Pressing with his left knee, the defender applies painful neck control.

and grinding his knees and shins on him to monitor, control, check, pin, or punish him. Figure 130 shows how the defender is able to pin and control his opponent's legs. After seating, the defender simply rotates his hips counterclockwise and uses his right leg to press on his opponent's legs, preventing him from using his legs in a counterattack. By rotating his hips the other way, the defender can drive his left knee into his opponent's head or neck, dissuading him from further resistance (fig. 131). All of this is possible because the defender first dropped to a squatting horse.

Passive Seating

Where active seating works from the squatting horse and brings the defender's weapons directly to bear on his opponent, passive seating uses the standing horse and brings the opponent against the anvil formed by the defender's leg/knee. For example, when the defender seats in a horse, he can break his attacker over an anvil formed by the defender's knee (fig. 132). The knee does not actively pursue the foe. Rather, it is the stone that the attacker is hurled against. This is passive seating. A similar example has the defender sitting squarely in a horse while locking the attacker's arm over the fulcrum formed by the defender's thigh (fig. 133).

Seating without Direct Impact

Seating, applied indirectly, uses the same principle shown above, but without direct impact on the opponent (neither actively nor passively). A good example of indirect seating has the defender pulling his opponent down by suddenly dropping his weight.

The next sequence takes off with the defender having just whipped his opponent backward. Continuing the motion begun by the whip (fig. 134), but changing the direction, the defender now rotates counterclockwise and seats, pulling his adversary down forcefully. This example of "seating without direct impact" is so named because the movement is performed without an accompnying strike. However, this does not mean that it is without impact. Certainly, slamming the assailant into the ground has an impact on him. Following up with active seating, the defender sticks to his assailant, pressing his shins against him, controlling him on the ground (fig. 135).

Figure 132: Passive seating with the attacker impaled on the defender's right knee.

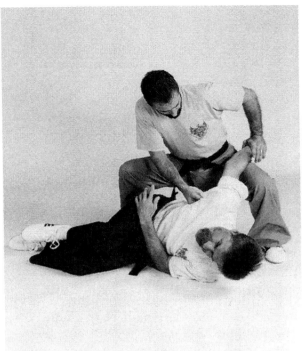

Figure 133: Passive seating with the defender using the fulcrum of his left thigh to apply a painful arm bar.

Figure 134: Pulling the opponent down from behind.

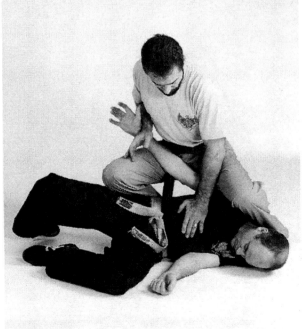

Figure 135: Using the squatting horse to control an opponent.

It is important to remember that when seating and sticking to your opponent, you press your shins and knees on the attacker. Where possible, keep your feet tucked slightly under him—close, but not so close that you become pinned yourself.

Seating as an Evasive Maneuver

The preceding examples show seating used with adhesion. However, seating's use of the quick drop is also helpful elsewhere—when avoiding a blow, for example.

In this example of evading an incoming punch, the defender uses the seating principle to suddenly drop into a low horse stance. The sudden drop moves the attacker's intended target (usually the head) from its initial position (fig. 136). The maneuver is executed with a simultaneous block or deflection to ensure that the incoming blow misses its mark. Any self-respecting kuntaoer would add a simultaneous strike to this maneuver.

The key to this seating method is surprisingly simple: you simply pick up your feet! The fastest way to effect a sudden drop in your position is to pick up your feet and let gravity do

Figure 136: Using seating to avoid the attacker's punch and simultaneously strike his groin.

The beginning position.　　Picking up the feet . . .　　. . . and letting gravity do the rest.

70

the rest. The illustration shows this. From his initial, most upright position, the fighter picks up his feet. Keeping his feet in their elevated position, he simply allows gravity to pull him quickly down to his new (and now lower) end position.

Note that from this position the defender must be prepared to strike and move quickly. He must press his attack because, although his move has taken him out of the line of fire, his position still has him well within the effective range of his opponent's weapons. In contrast to most other arts, in Indonesian arts, fighting from a position this low and close to the opponent is an advantage for the well-trained fighter. Seating to evade an attack takes you out of harm's way without sacrificing the opportunity to counterattack.

Pulling It Together

Let's look at an example of seating that uses all the applications: active, passive, indirect, and as an evasive maneuver. We start with a response to a two-handed lapel grab.

The defender's initial reaction is an open-hand strike to his assailant's face, as in Figure 137. (The strike can be an attack to his eyes or a heavy-handed slap.) From there, both arms drape over the opponent's (fig. 138), and the defender drops like a dead weight, as in Figure 139. (This is the same method used in our example of seating as an evasive maneuver. As such, it is important to remember not to force the sudden weight shift by jumping or stomping. Remember, weight is dropped by simply raising the feet and letting gravity do the rest.) This is also indirect seating because the defender is seating without any direct impact—active or passive.

Figure 137: A painful distraction.

Figure 138: Defender draping both arms over his opponent's.

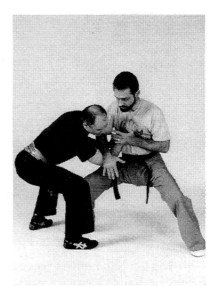

Figure 139: Seated in a squatting horse.

Figure 140: Defender's left hand feeding opponent's arm to the right.

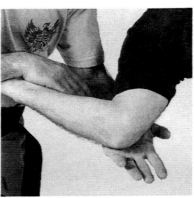

Figure 141: Close-up of the defender's hand placement.

Figure 142: Casting off opponent's arms.

Figure 143: The defender preparing to take his opponent down.

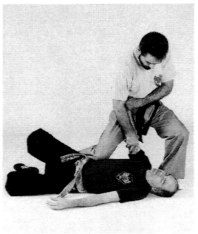

Figure 144: Active seating has the defender pinning his opponent to the ground with his right shin.

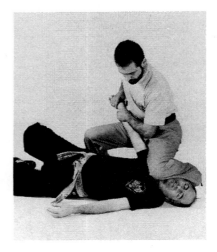

Figure 145: Passive seating, using the arm bar combined with active seating, pressing on opponent's neck.

His left hand now drives or whips his opponent's arms to the defender's right (fig. 140). (The defender's hands are at or near his opponent's right elbow, as shown in fig. 141.) This movement directs his opponent's arms in a shallow downward-to-upward arc that turns him counterclockwise (fig. 142).

This new position makes it easy for the defender to attach his right hand to his opponent's head and drive him into the ground (fig. 143). Sticking with him as he goes down, the defender applies active seating, pinning his assailant to the ground (fig. 144). Finally, finishing with an example of passive and active seating, the defender traps the assailant's right arm and presses it against his own right thigh (fig. 145) as he simultaneously presses his left shin against his opponent's neck. This technique provides an excellent example of the seating principle and its various applications in combat.

Seating is a versatile and useful tool. By using it actively, passively, indirectly, and as an evasive maneuver, the Indonesian fighter is able to bring his opponent down and stick with him all the way to the ground. There he can monitor, control, check, pin, or punish him.

Chapter 7

Leg Maneuvers

The public's fascination with Asian martial arts comes largely from those arts' unashamed use of the feet in fighting. Unlike Western boxing, Asian fighting arts place as much importance on training and conditioning the feet as weapons as they do training and conditioning the hands. However, despite the popularity and proliferation of these arts, very few instructors teach their students to use their hands and feet together in simultaneous combinations. (The operative words here are *together* and *simultaneous*.)

It is axiomatic that anyone using long-range kicking techniques will have difficulty using his hands and feet simultaneously because of the obvious difference in arm and leg length. Even Filipino fighters, well known for their excellent footwork, often fight from positions that (because of their emphasis on weapons) keep them too far from their opponent's legs to take maximum advantage of even their highly developed leg skills. Both long-range kicking and the emphasis on weapon skills are effective, and both have their place in the martial artist's arsenal, but there is yet another level of development that is rarely taught and little understood: leg locking.

LEG LOCKING: A SYMPHONY OF DESTRUCTION

Indonesian martial arts possess a formidable array of exotic weaponry, and, although not often observed, they also have a suite of their own unique aerial and long-range fighting tactics. However, in North America their appeal has been largely in their empty-hand, close-quarter combat skills.

Figure 146

Figure 147

Figure 148

Figure 149

Figure 150

Figure 151

Figure 152

When reach-extending weaponry and long-range kicking techniques are unavailable, the fighter trained in the Indonesian arts is still a formidable foe. Moving in closer than most of us would dare, the Indonesian fighter uses both his legs and arms to orchestrate a simultaneous symphony of destruction.

To see how leg-locking principles are used in combat, let's begin with a technique that, although very effective, is surprisingly simple. The absence of "flash" in the technique allows us to focus on the leg action.

The attacker opens with a right haymaker punch. The defender's initial move is an aggressive one. Attacking his assailant's outstretched arm, the defender uses a double-arm block that smothers the incoming punch, while simultaneously driving a right elbow or forearm into his attacker's chest (fig. 146). As if discarding the offending arm, both hands (positioned at the opponent's right arm) explode in a downward arc, violently slinging the opponent's arm to the defender's right. The force of this action turns even the strongest opponent completely around (figs. 147 through 150). From this position, the attacker is easily sent to the ground (figs. 151 and 152).

As long as we confine our focus to upper body defensive tactics (excluding leg work), it makes little difference which foot the attacker leads with. So, for the moment, let us continue to work against an opponent who punches using the classical Asian punching method.[1]

The technique just described is effective. However, it is still limited because the defender has done the following:

1. used only upper-body weapons in his defense
2. left his attacker a means of escape (by yielding to the spin and stepping out)
3. left the attacker free to counterattack with a kick

With the introduction of some basic leg control, the defender can significantly improve the effectiveness of the technique. By planting his right foot and shin firmly against the attacker's lead leg, the defender makes it impossible for his assailant to move his leg (offensively or defensively) without the defender's knowledge. The leg lock prevents the unimpeded use of the attacker's right knee as a counterattacking weapon while simultaneously reducing his chance of escape.

With this simple leg lock, the same technique takes on a new dimension. It begins as before: the attacker throws a right haymaker punch, and the defender stops his charge with a double-arm block and simultaneous right elbow strike. This time, however—as part of his initial response—the defender locks his lead leg against his opponent's right shin (fig. 153).

The defender's right foot is placed inside and slightly behind the attacker's right leg. Ideally, this arch is wedged tightly against the attacker's heel, making his withdrawal very difficult. The defender's shin lies across and along the attacker's, crossing it at a slight diagonal. This keeps the defender's knee outside of his attacker's (fig. 154). Pressure exerted against the attacker's leg may be directed either straight back against his knee (hyperextending it) or rotated clockwise, stressing the inside of his right knee.

Again, with an explosive downward sweeping action, the defender discards his opponent's arm—a move that causes the attacker to spin violently counterclockwise. However, with the assailant's right leg locked in place, the same spin is much more effective, for it traps and buckles his leg (fig. 155). And this is only the beginning, for the assailant's already precarious position only worsens in the follow-up.

Figure 153

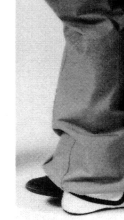

Figure 154

Figure 155

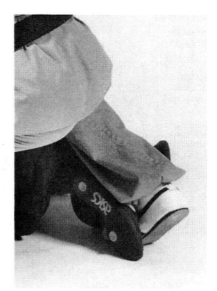

Figure 156

Figure 157: Trapping assailant's right leg pins and neutralizes his left leg.

Figure 158: Close-up of trapped leg.

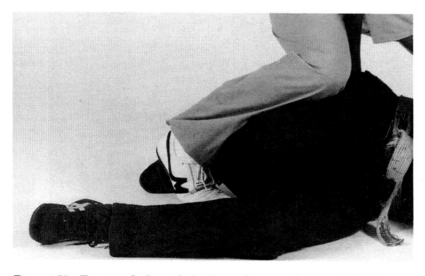

Figure 159: Trapping the leg with the foot and pinning the leg with the shin.

As he is taken down, the assailant finds no avenue of escape. Had his legs been free, he might have rolled over backward to recover, but the defender denies him that option by locking his right leg (figs. 156 through 159). Using a basic leg lock has dramatically improved this defense.

In Opposite Leads

Most martial art schools teach punching like this: starting from a left-lead stance, the student advances with his right foot to a right-lead stance and delivers a right (horizontal fist) lunge punch. However, most American fighters fight from the Western boxing posture (one that punches with the right hand, but from a left-lead stance). I will not address the pros and cons of these punching methods except to say that this small variation makes a very big difference when the leg-locking maneuver is used. Let's revisit the last technique, but this time we will have the attacker assume the more orthodox left-lead stance. The defense itself is identical to the two previous versions—only the attack has changed.

Figure 160: Assailant throws an American-style right punch from a left lead (his left hand is also cocked, ready to strike).

Figure 161: Locking the assailant's near left leg means that the defender has only to whip his opponent a small distance to severely twist him.

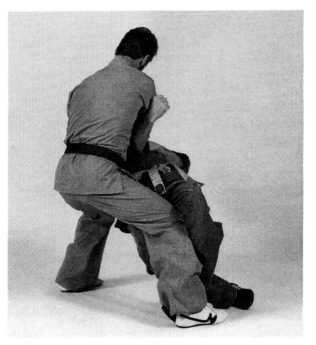

Figure 162: Badly twisted, the assailant is helpless to resist being taken to the ground.

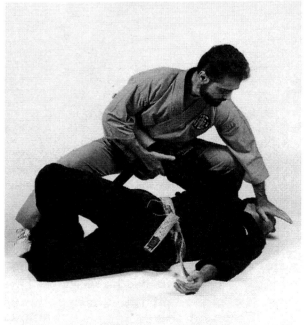

Figure 163: Trapping his opponent's left leg effectively neutralizes both legs.

Figure 160 shows the defender's initial double-hand block and simultaneous elbow/forearm strike. (Note that here the defender's right leg is already locked outside his opponent's leading left leg.) In Figure 161, the defender slings his assailant's arm down and out to the right. This time, however, with the attacker now in a left lead, the counterclockwise spin is doubly devastating. As the assailant is taken down (fig. 162), both of his legs are pinned, as shown in Figure 163 (effectively eliminating any counterattack he may mount using his legs). From this position the opponent has far fewer escape options than he had before the leg lock was applied.

LEG-LOCK TRAINING: BASIC DRILLS

Instinctive use of leg locks can be acquired by incorporating them into regular practice of static self-defense techniques; however, experience has shown us that there are better and faster ways to develop these skills. The method we use in our school is a series of continuous-action two-man drills.

Although two-man flow drills are explained in detail in the next chapter, a brief description of how they are used here is in order. These two-man drills (where one player advances, applying the locks, as the other withdraws and defends) dynamically develop an awareness of weapons and targets while ingraining the reflexes necessary to use them and attack them. A variety of drills exist, but here are basic ones that you can learn and apply quickly. (Since these are training drills, and to make the sequences easier to follow, the participants are referred to as Player A and Player B.)

Figure 164: Drill number one. Left legs locked, shin to shin.

Figure 165: Right foot advances to right leg shin-to-shin lock.

Drill Number One

The first drill is used when facing an individual in a "like" lead (both players are in the same lead: either right-facing-right or left-facing-left). In this sequence, both players begin with their left legs engaged or locked together. Both have their feet turned inward at approximately 45 degrees, with contact being made with both the foot and shin (fig. 164).

Player A begins by applying pressure and grinding his left shin against his partner's. At this, Player B retreats, stepping back with his left leg; he is now in a right lead. Filling the void B's withdrawal creates, Player A advances, stepping forward with his right leg and locking his right foot and shin firmly against B's (fig. 165). As before, Player A applies pressure to his partner's right shin with his (now) forward right leg. Again, Player B withdraws his leg, and the sequence is repeated. Player B retreats until he runs out of floor space, then he takes the offensive, forcing Player A, in turn, to retreat back across the floor.

Figure 166: Drill number two. Begin with left leg locked outside your partner's right.

Figure 167: After advancing, the right foot is outside and behind your partner's left.

Drill Number Two

The first drill is simple enough, and the second works much like it, except that both players begin in opposite leads—Player A's leading left leg is locked against the outside of his partner's right.

As before, Player A's left foot is turned inward 45 degrees, but this time his arch is jammed tightly against his partner's heel (fig. 166). His shin also presses firmly against the outside of Player B's calf. From this position, Player A applies pressure to his partner's right leg with his left, and Player B begins his withdrawal.

As Player B withdraws, Player A advances, locking his right foot and shin firmly behind and outside his partner's (now) forward left, as in Figure 167. (It is important to remember that I am addressing only leg action here; in practice, each drill also incorporates upper-body movement to further check and control the opponent.)

Battle Chess

Before going much further, you need to know something about when and where these leg-locking tactics are applied. This requires a little insight into fight dynamics.

Fights can be broken down into three stages. Borrowing terminology from the world of chess, those stages are: early, middle, and late game. In reality, most one-on-one altercations rarely last more than a few seconds. Consequently, few fights ever reach the middle- or late-game stages. However, in multiman confrontations, fights often move into these latter phases. Understanding early-, middle-, and late-game tactics, then, is critical to the proper use of these leg maneuvers. Each maneuver teaches principles and tactics that apply specifically to one stage or another.

For example, the first drill teaches a tactic that works well in all three stages of the game. Most of the other leg maneuvers are much more suited to the middle or late game. The first one's usefulness in the early game, however, distinguishes it from the other drills.

Under certain conditions, the leg-locking maneuver used in the second drill also works well in the early game. Against a left jab, for example, the tactic taught in the second drill is easy to incorporate into the defender's initial response. You can see that proper application of these tactics requires a good sense of timing and fight dynamics. But look for a moment at some other differences between these first two drills and their applications.

The second drill is superior to the first, both defensively and offensively. In the first drill, both players have the same legs locked together (right-to-right or left-to-left). Because of this, each has a nearly equal chance of applying the tactic against the other. In this drill, the player initiating the shin-to-shin clash (in our case, the defender) does have a slight advantage.[2] However, if the defender is not aggressive enough, his opponent may steal this advantage by applying the maneuver first.

The tactic employed in the second drill, however, gives a much stronger advantage to the defender whose leg is on the outside. The player holding the outside position can exert much more pressure than the player on the inside can resist. This point alone makes the maneuver the superior tactic. But the tactics taught in the first two drills do not cover everything. Middle- and late-game skills are also needed. For those skills we turn to drills number three and four.

Figure 168: Drill three begins with the right leg outside your partner's right.

Figure 169: After advance, the left leg is locked behind your partner's left.

Drill Number Three

Drills one and two are common to both kuntao and silat (although the two arts apply them differently). However, drills three and four are rooted firmly in kuntao, specifically in the art of pakua.

Like the first drill, the third begins with both players' right (like) legs locked together. This time, however, Player A's right foot is positioned outside his partner's. It is turned outward 45 degrees, and the foot and shin are in firm contact with Player B's leg (fig. 168).

As in the previous examples, a slight bend of A's right knee applies grinding pressure to his partner's lead (right) leg. As Player A presses, Player B withdraws to a left lead (fig. 169), and the repetition begins—working back and forth, in turn. (Execution of this maneuver is common in Chinese systems, although it is often applied or interpreted as a foot-stomp or shin-slide.)

Figure 170: Drill four begins with the left shin locked inside your partner's right.

Figure 171: Right-shin-on-left shin-to-shin lock.

Drill Number Four

This drill uses the same foot position as the previous one, only this one is practiced from opposite leads—that is, Player A's right leg is still turned outward 45 degrees, but this time it is locked inside Player B's left (figs. 170 and 171). This drill is more difficult than the preceding ones because additional footwork and angling are required as you advance on your partner; however, once mastered, the drill provides an excellent example of lower- and upper-body mechanics working in effective concert.

Figure 172: Drill five begins with drill number one shin-to-shin lock.

Figure 173: Right crosses in front of left to secure a right-to-right, shin-to-calf lock.

Drill Number Five—Combining Drills One and Three

Drills five and six are simply combinations of drills one and three, and two and four, respectively. Like drill number one, the fifth drill begins with both players in the same lead. They begin with their lead left legs engaged; their feet are turned inward approximately 45 degrees, and contact is made with both the foot and shin (fig. 172).

Player A applies grinding pressure with his left shin to his partner's left leg. Player B retreats. Filling the void B's withdrawal creates, Player A advances—only this time, he advances his right foot, crossing it in front of his left and planting his right shin against the calf of his partner's now forward right leg (fig. 173). As in the third drill, Player A applies pressure to his partner's right with his (now) forward right leg, and Player B, continuing the drill, withdraws.

An important difference in this drill is the fact that Player A's lead does not change as he advances. Instead, he remains in the same lead through each iteration. Unlike the first four drills—drills that by their alternating nature develop equal proficiency on both sides (left and right)—this drill must be practiced with the players starting it in a right-to-right lock as well as in a left-to-left.

Figure 174: Begins as drill number two with a left-on-right shin-to-calf lock.

Figure 175: Move to right-on-left shin-to-shin lock.

Drill Number Six—Combining Drills Two and Four

Drill six begins like drill number two: that is, both players are in opposite or different leads. Player A's leading left leg is locked against the outside (or calf side) of his partner's right. As in the second drill, Player A has his left foot turned in 45 degrees with his arch jammed tightly against his partner's heel (fig. 174) and his shin pressed firmly against the outside of Player B's calf. From this position, Player A applies pressure to his partner's right leg, and his partner withdraws.

As Player B withdraws, Player A advances, crossing in front of his left and locking his right shin against his partner's left shin (fig. 175). As in the fourth drill, Player A applies pressure to his partner's left shin and his partner withdraws. Like drill number five, the drill continues with Player A remaining in the same lead and his partner changing leads with each retreat.

Drills five and six give you a hint of how, just as words and sentences are formed using a few letters of the alphabet and some basic rules, drills are formed using a few basic leg movements and some basic rules. The possibilities are limited only by your imagination.

Now some may look at these drills and say, "I would never fight from such a position," and I would be the first to agree that I would not intentionally choose such a position. I ask you to remember, however, that these are only training drills. As such, their purpose is not to serve as actual self-defense techniques. Rather, these drills provide the coordination and sensitivity that contribute to and enhance already good self-defense skills.

Figure 176: The face-off.

Figure 177: Right flip-kick.

Bridging the Gap

The following photo sequence illustrates a situation where the lock is positioned in the early game but not fully exploited until the end of the fight. In Figure 176, the attacker (in black) has already taken a swing at the defender, and both fighters now face each other with their guards up and their right sides forward.

The defender (on the left) begins by firing a right flip kick[3] to the attacker's groin (fig. 177). Recovering from the flip kick, the attacker plants his right foot directly on the floor—up against the inside of the defender's right foot.

Figure 178

Figure 179

Figure 180

The defender follows the flip kick with a left reverse punch to his opponent's ribs (fig. 178). (He may set up the left reverse punch with a right backfist or by having his right hand check or pin his opponent's lead arm.) Following this, the defender clears his attacker's right arm using a two-hand (left, right) combination (figs. 179 and 180) and advances on his opponent by stepping forward with his left leg, as shown in Figure 181. (In the two-hand combination shown in Figures 179 and 180, the defender's left hand is in the thumb-up position. His right thumb is pointing down.)

The left-step advance places great pressure on the attacker's lead right leg. Bending at the hip to save his knee, he cannot help but place his face squarely in the path of the defender's shearing right horizontal elbow.

Figure 181

Figure 182

Figure 183

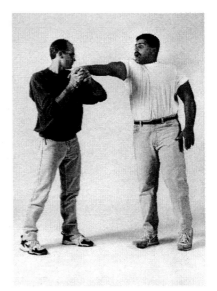

Figure 184

Effective Is Simple

Drills like these provide excellent practice, but without some common sense one loses sight of the goal—namely, immobilization, control, or destruction of an opponent's legs. The drills make us aware of weapons and targets and help us develop the skill to use them. However, in many actual combat situations there may be a simpler way to accomplish this goal: *step on your assailant's foot.* Sounds too simple, I know, but let's look at an example—a handshake squeeze.

One can effectively turn the tables on an overly aggressive hand-shaker and regain quick control with this simple maneuver (fig. 182). First, pull your grasped hand back to your right hip (fig. 183). Then, with your left hand, clamping against the back of his right, you lift his hand to face height, as in Figure 184. (Your opponent's arm is straight, with his palm open toward you and his fingers pointing down.) You can now walk the individual to the nearest door, or otherwise persuade him to behave.

Figure 185

Figure 186

Figure 187: The same technique as Figures 182 through 184, only this time the assailant's foot is pinned.

The weakness in this technique is that your antagonist may walk faster than you and walk right out of your grasp. Worse, he can still use his legs as weapons against you if his aggression escalates. Foot-pinning improves this technique enormously. After pulling your opponent's right hand back to your hip (figs. 185 and 186), you step on his lead foot with your left. With the application of your grasp-and-lift, there is nowhere for the gorilla to go, and his pain is increased substantially (fig. 187). The addition of this simple foot-pin to our upper-body action makes a day-and-night difference.

Some will find leg-locking and foot-pinning difficult. It can be frustrating, and some may be tempted to throw up their hands and walk away (providing, of course, that they can extricate their feet). Seriously though, advanced martial art training involves unlearning old habits and replacing them with new ones. For most of our lives we're taught to say "excuse me" when we step on someone's foot, and then we get off that foot quickly. We also shift our thinking to our feet when someone steps on one of ours. It takes time to replace that "excuse me" reflex and the tendency to shift our focus to our feet when stepped on with habits that better serve our self-defense goals. With a little practice, the reflexes developed by these drills become automatic, and in no time at all, you will find yourself locking legs and stepping on feet without a second thought.

HOLISTIC COMBAT

Indonesian players do much, much more with their feet than just what is presented here. For example, harimau (tiger) silat practitioners fight very low to the ground and use their legs in sweeping, hooking, and kicking actions that can demolish an enemy who fights in an upright position. Maduran[4] pamur silat fighters, on the other hand, are highly acrobatic and deliver high kicks from a variety of positions. Considering the number of different Indonesian systems, it must be realized that what is covered here is only a small fraction of the leg skills Indonesia's arts offer.

If you have not already noticed it, leg locking is tactical application of the adhesion principle in the lower art. Practice and proper application of these drills and the adhesion principle help the fighter truly use his hands and feet together in simultaneous combinations. The result can be a symphony of destruction played on the instruments of the upper and the lower arts.

Indonesian martial arts take a holistic approach to personal combat. For example, one can fight with either hands *or* feet. One can even fight with hands and *then* feet (or feet and then hands). But to be really effective, one should learn to fight with hands *and* feet, thereby using the whole body. It is largely because of their holistic approach to personal combat that Indonesian martial arts are some of the most effective fighting systems in the world.

NOTES

1. The classical Asian punching method is one that uses a lunge punch—throwing a right punch with the right foot leading. It is basically a training punch designed to help the student learn basic punching theory.
2. In any shin-to-shin clash, the one driving his shin into the other has the advantage because: a) He has momentum on his side, and b) The individual being struck is usually caught with his leg somewhat immobilized. This is proven frequently by those who break bats with their shins. They perform this feat by striking the bats with their shins and not by striking their shins with the bat.
3. A flip kick is similar to a classical roundhouse kick, except that the knee stays down (below the foot) throughout the movement, and the striking surface is the top-outside portion of the foot. Another difference between the two kicks is that the flip kick recovers on the floor. The classical roundhouse kick recovers at the initial chamber position. Because of the flip kick's recovery position, it is well suited to leg-locking follow-ups.
4. Madura is an island off the northeast coast of Java.

Chapter 8

Peanut Brittle

Although the focus of this book is on Indonesian arts, I feel it is important to introduce you to certain other Southeast Asian influences. In this chapter, you will see training methods that are common to another culture—one that is, in many ways, similar to Indonesia: the Philippines. The Philippines, like Indonesia, has resisted many invaders, freed herself from colonial rule, and stands today as a nation proud of its diverse, multicultural heritage.

As with Indonesia, the Filipino struggle for freedom and national identity has produced systems of combat that are highly respected among martial artists everywhere. The cultural similarities between Indonesia and the Philippines make for a union that is as natural as peanuts and caramelized sugar. (For those unfamiliar with that culinary combination, it's called peanut brittle.)

From my perspective, I see the tactics, skills, and principles found in the Indonesian arts as the peanuts in the recipe—delightful nuggets; meaty and rich.[1] The flow and sensitivity training methods for which Filipino martial arts are renowned are the brittle—that flavorful, sweet, and smooth sauce that binds it all together, resulting in something that is better than either component by itself. As you will see, both cultures complement each other, and together they better help us meet the second stated objective of this book, which is *to take existing training methods and develop drills and tools that will help us assimilate the fighting principles found in Indonesian arts.* On that note, we begin with a basic flow drill.

KILAP HANDS: A BASIC FLOW DRILL

A basic flow drill common to Filipino martial arts is the two-man continuous-action training exercise called *hubud lubud.* In this country, such drills are known generally as flow or sensitivity drills. However, with the introduction and infusion of Indonesian weapons and striking methods (the nuggets) to the basic two-man flow (the brittle), I have taken to calling these drills "*kilap* hand drills."[2]

These two-man multihand training methods develop combination-type reactions to a variety of attacks, both weaponed and empty-handed. Moreover, their continuous nature makes them excellent vehicles for learning and ingraining various Indonesian tactics. Let's begin with a brief look at the basic flow drill as applied to empty-hand training.

Figure 188: Block-right's initial left hand interception.

Figure 189: Right hand displaces the left by sliding down the arm.

The Block-Right Flow Drill

This first drill uses the blocking method described in Chapter 1: block-right. The drill begins with Player A (on the left in fig. 188) executing a right vertical punch to Player B's face. Player B (on the right) intercepts the incoming blow with his left hand. Immediately following this interception, Player B's right hand, coming from a position below his left hand, rises to provide the bulk of the support needed for the block (fig. 189).

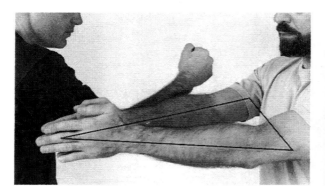

Figure 190: The triangle (wedge).

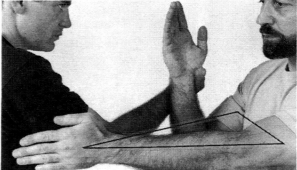

Figure 191: The right hand traverses the right side of the triangle.

Although substantially the same as the block-right movement you saw in Chapter 1, this execution differs in one respect: the second count of the maneuver has Player B's right hand sliding along Player A's arm, back toward Player B, rather than "out" to his right. Mentally, picture this as if you are shaving the outside of your partner's arm with the back of your arm. Visualize the line you follow as a triangle in front of you. You form an isosceles triangle as you straighten your arms in front of you and bring your hands together (fig. 190). In this execution of block-right, your right arm travels down the right length of the triangle (fig. 191). In Chapter 1, block-right's purpose was simple deflection of a punch. Here, as part of a block-and-counter combination, it also positions the defender's right hand for quick execution of a counterstrike.

Figure 192: The left hand slaps down (clears) Player A's right arm.

Figure 193: The left hand's clearing action pulls Player A into Player B's right punch.

With the blocking portion of the drill completed, Player B now clears Player A's right arm by slapping it down with his left hand (fig. 192). This action clears away Player A's hand and, at the same time, pulls his face into Player B's right counterpunch, as shown in Figure 193. (Player B's punch is the fourth count of this four-count drill). To effect the pulling-in of Player A, Player B's downward slap must be close to A's elbow. The reason for this was briefly discussed in the Introduction, but as a reminder, the defender's clearing hand is placed at his opponent's elbow because there, the natural folding action of the arm provides a handle for the defender to use to pull his opponent to him.[3] Figure 193 shows the effect of the pulling action. As Player B executes his right punch to his partner's face, Player A intercepts the punch with his left hand, beginning his four-count response. This is the basic drill for the right side.

On the left side, the flow is similar in that it has four counts; however, the hand positions are different. The drill for the left side is different because it uses block-left as its method of interception and deflection.

Figure 194: Block-left's initial right hand deflection.

Figure 195: The left hand displaces Player B's right (deflecting) hand.

The Block-Left Flow Drill

In the block-left version, Player A (the player on the right this time) begins the drill with a left punch to his partner's face. While Player A punches, Player B's right hand intercepts the punch at or near his partner's elbow, parrying it inward (fig. 194). This allows Player B to slip outside A's punch. Meanwhile, Player B's left hand—already chambered near his right shoulder—now displaces and reinforces his initial (right-hand) interception, as in Figure 195. (All of this should be familiar to you because of our discussion of the block-left maneuver in Chapter 1.)

Immediately following the left-hand displacement, Player B executes a right poke to Player A's eye, as in Figure 196. (In the drill we touch the left eyebrow to simulate the strike.) This right-hand eye poke is followed by a left vertical punch to Player A's face and a simultaneous slapping down of A's left arm by B's right hand (fig. 197). As with the right-side maneuver, the downward slap pulls Player A into a punch that is already accelerating to the target—his face.[4]

These two basic drills take blocking methods that are developed from Indonesian arts (block-right and block-left) and seamlessly incorporate them into simple flow drills. The continuous nature of the drills allows the student to receive many times more practice, feedback, and reinforcement of the basic principles he is learning than he might normally receive using other training methods. The feedback each player receives on each iteration provides many opportunities for real-time correction.

Figure 196: Right eye poke.

Figure 197: Left punch.

Figure 198: Block-right flow drill—count number one.

Figure 199: Block-right's count number two.

The American Contribution: The Switch

The similarity in Filipino and Indonesian cultures is the primary reason Filipino training methods work as well as they do in transmitting Indonesian fighting principles, tactics, and striking methods. The asymmetrical approach (practicing it differently on each side) is, on the other hand, an American contribution. Given two ways of doing anything, most of us develop a preference for one over the other. The result of that natural preference is the practice of one method more than the other. This leads to a disparity in skill levels when both methods are compared.

By practicing one entry method on the right side and the other on the left, asymmetrically, we bring the student closer to equality in training. Further, when these flow drills are practiced in a way that allows the players to transition smoothly from one drill to the other, each player becomes completely comfortable with both left and right training methods. (In self-defense, the importance of the ability to adapt and switch from one tactic or method to another cannot be overstated; it is critical.) Here is an example of a switch using the two flow drills we have just seen.

Figure 200: Count number three.

Figure 201: Count number four.

In this example, we will move quickly through the block-right flow drill, through a switch (which I will describe in detail), and then quickly through the block-left flow. Figures 198 through 201 show Player A's interception of Player B's punch, his clearing of B's arm, and A's counterpunch. (Imagine that this drill has continued through several iterations.) Player B now initiates a three-count switch sequence.

Figure 202: Player B's left hand intercepts Player A's right punch (A's fourth count).

Figure 203: Player B's right parries and traps Player A's hand.

As Player A executes his fourth-count punch, Player B intercepts that punch with his left hand as though he were continuing the drill (fig. 202). Player B's right hand comes from below his left (as before) and completes the block (fig. 203). This time, however, instead of clearing A's punch with his left hand (as in the normal four-count flow), Player B's right hand grasps A's arm (fig. 204) as he simultaneously executes a left punch to A's face (fig. 205). Player B's punch is the third count of his half of the switch sequence. As you will see in Figures 206 through 208, Player A responds to B's left punch with his three-count answer that completes the switch and resynchronizes both players for the left-side flow.

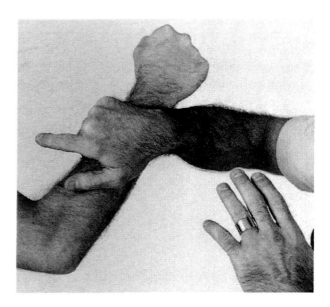

Figure 204: Close-up of parry-turned-trap.

Figure 205: Player B executes a right vertical punch to Player A's face.

Figure 206: Player A's left hand intercepts Player B's left punch.

Responding to Player B's switch, Player A intercepts B's left punch with a left-hand inward deflection moving from his left to right (fig. 206), followed by a right outward parry that also moves left to right (fig. 207). Completing his half of the switch, Player A executes his own left vertical punch to B's face (fig. 208). At this point both players are positioned to commence the block-left flow drill.

Figure 208: Player A's left vertical punch to Player B's face.

Figure 209: Player B's right-hand intercept.

Figure 210: Player B's left-hand displacement.

Figure 211: Right eye poke.

Figure 212: Left vertical punch.

Player B begins the block-left flow drill by intercepting A's left punch near A's left elbow (fig. 209), displacing and supporting his own left deflection with his right hand (fig. 210), executing a right eye poke to Player A (fig. 211), and, finally, executing a left vertical punch to A's face (fig. 212). (This is Player B's fourth and final count of the block-left flow.)

I will not spend any more time on the switch here, but one thing should not be lost in all of this. The one initiating the switch may, after having his switch answered, immediately switch again. This double-switch only means that after switching (and reswitching) both players end up on the same side they were on when the first player began the switch.

There are many possible hand combinations that can be worked into flow drills like these; however, I will not elaborate on them here since the intent is to focus on learning Indonesian principles.

In the following section you will see the same flow drill, but now you will see it as it is played with tactics and weapons from pentjak silat and Chinese kuntao.[5]

Figure 213: Left hand intercepts Player A's elbow.

Figure 214: Right outward parry against back of Player A's triceps.

Figure 215: Shearing elbow strike.

SHIFTING TO STRIKE MODE

Performing the drills you have just seen in strike mode means that instead of using block-right and block-left, we use strike-right and strike-left. Likewise, the switches also run in strike mode, with the second count of the three-count switch being a strike to our partner's face or eyes. I point this out because throughout the remainder of this chapter all the drills will be executed in strike mode.[6]

Exquisite Elbows

Perhaps the most recognizable characteristic of Indonesian martial arts is its extensive use of elbows.[7] It is the Indonesian fighter's unashamed and exquisite use of elbows that makes his the infighter's art of choice. Most of us view elbows as short-range weapons; however, Indonesians are so expert with them that they break down elbow strikes into short-, middle-, and long-range. Let's see how these devastating elbow strikes can be incorporated into our flow drills.

We begin with Player A (on the left) executing a right horizontal elbow to Player B's head. Player B checks the incoming elbow with his left hand (fig. 213). This check is more than just a save-your-face maneuver. Although it may not stop a full-force elbow, executing it aggressively—that is, attacking—should slow your opponent's strike down. Even if your check only slows down the strike a small amount, you are still better off catching an elbow in the hand than failing to check it at all.

Following the initial interception by the left hand, Player B's right hand, coming from beneath the left, pops up behind the attacking elbow and redirects it to Player B's right (fig. 214).[8] From there, B's right hand turns over to a palm-down position, momentarily trapping A's right arm. Simultaneously, Player B drives the point of his left elbow into Player A's right triceps (fig. 215). You should recognize this as the shearing strike you saw in Chapter 5. It is driven deeply into Player A's arm bone, producing pain and incapacitating his arm. From the elbow strike, Player B's left hand now slaps A's elbow down (fig. 216), clearing the way for B to finish the flow with a right horizontal elbow strike of his own (fig. 217). With that, Player A begins his part of the flow.

Figure 216: Clearing Player A's right arm.

Figure 217: Player B's horizontal elbow.

Adding the Hacksaw

With a little imagination we can extend this drill by inserting a hacksaw forearm to the flow. (This will change the drill from a four- to a five-count flow.)

As before, Player A begins with a right horizontal elbow attack to B's head. Again, Player B checks the incoming elbow with his left hand (fig. 218). Now we insert the hacksaw forearm strike. The hacksaw (count two) grinds through Player A's ribs (fig. 219). The drill continues with Player B's right hand coming from its ending position in the preceding hacksaw blow and reappearing behind the attacking elbow to redirect it to Player B's right (count three). It should be noted that in the redirection of the attacking elbow, it is the radial or thumb-side bone in the forearm that strikes the back of Player A's upper arm (fig. 220). The rest of the drill is the same as before: Player B's left hand slapping the elbow down, followed by a right horizontal elbow attack to Player A's head.

Figure 218: Intercepting the elbow.

Figure 219: Right hacksaw-forearm strike to Player A's ribs.

Figure 220: Right parry clears Player A's arm striking his triceps.

Figure 221: Intercepting the punch.

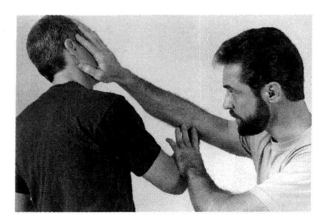

Figure 222: Covering the attacker's eyes.

So far, the flow drills have incorporated the principles of shearing and adhesion—tactics and weapons common to Indonesian fighters. The next drill injects some leg action as well.

Leg Attacks

Drills incorporating leg attacks are longer (contain more counts) than the preceding drills. Here, we begin with a six-count strike-mode flow. Using strike-right, Player A intercepts B's right punch with his left hand (fig. 221) and immediately executes a quick right-hand strike to Player B's face (fig. 222). This is not an eye poke, although pain to an attacker's eye is a likely result. As was pointed out earlier (see Chapters 1 and 4), in application this hand strike, although very

Figure 223: The strike must cover the opponent's eyes. This prevents his seeing (and countering) your next move.

relaxed, is neither light nor airy, for it lands like a heavy wet towel. In the drill (and in the movement's application) the striking hand remains on (adheres to) Player B's face (fig. 223). The initial left deflecting hand stays with or on B's right arm. Both hands now apply forward pressure to B's upper body, shifting his weight off of his near leg and setting up the rest of this punishing defense.

Figure 224: Left knee strikes near leg.

Figure 225: Left foot kicks far leg.

Counts three and four have Player A's left knee driving into B's closest knee (fig. 224). Doubling up the left leg strike, all the while maintaining his forward upper-body pressure on Player B, Player A now drives a low left front kick into B's far leg—at or slightly above the ankle (fig. 225).

Figure 226: Shearing left vertical elbow.   **Figure 227:** Right punch finishes the drill.

Withdrawing his leg, Player A now removes his right hand from B's face and latches onto his right wrist.[9] As the left leg returns, Player A drives a left vertical elbow into his training partner's right arm (just above the elbow), as in Figure 226. Finishing his part of the drill, Player A's left hand clears B's right arm by slapping it down as he executes a right reverse punch of his own to B's face (fig. 227). With this, Player B intercepts A's punch and repeats the drill.

Combining Indonesian principles and weapons in this manner is both productive and enjoyable. However, extending any drill beyond six counts diminishes its effectiveness. A drill with more than six counts takes too long to complete. The benefit of the two-man drill lies in its quick and continuous back-and-forth play—the flow. Additional counts only diminish this benefit. Expanding these drills is better done by varying the elements introduced than by introducing more of them into a single drill.

RECIPE FOR SUCCESS

The cultural connection between Indonesia and the Philippines is undisputed, but nowhere is this connection more evident than in each nation's martial art development. Though they are similar in many ways, each maintains its own distinguishing characteristics and flavor. It is our recognition and affirmation of the similarities—an affirmation that acknowledges the effectiveness of both nation's arts—and the integration of each art's differences that allow us to fully assimilate principles inherent in both cultures' arts.

The drills presented in this chapter are undeniably an adaptation of Filipino training methods. To those excellent training methods, we inject principles and weapons common among Indonesian fighters. This "peanut brittle" approach results in a method of training that helps the student learn and practice timeless principles from Indonesia's martial arts in a very efficient and easy-to-learn way.

NOTES

1. Admittedly, my perspective is that of a student of Indo-Chinese arts. A Filipino martial artist, on the other hand, might see his art as the nuggets and the Indonesian arts as the sauce that binds the brittle. Either way, the natural union of the two is undeniable.

2. *Kilap* (pronounced KEE-lop) is an Indonesian word meaning "lightning." Kilap hand drills are training methods that help the practitioner develop lightning-fast hand (and elbow) combinations.

3. See the discussion around Figures 6-9 in the Introduction.

4. Applied in combat, this pulling downward slap is executed aggressively. However, when practicing the drill, we minimize this in order to maintain the flow.

5. Doubtless, there are similar tactics among Filipino adepts, but distinguishing between them all would require more space than this book permits.

6. As you will see in Chapter 9, strike-mode thinking is central to the other predominant fighting art practiced in Indonesia: Chinese kuntao.

7. This in no way minimizes the silat practitioner's extensive use of sophisticated and unique leg maneuvers.

8. In actual use, these first two actions are performed with body movement and angling to move the defender off the line of attack.

9. In combat, the left leg does not withdraw; it advances—possibly to follow with a leg-cutting sweep. However, to keep the drill flowing back and forth, adjustments must be made. In this case, the player withdraws the attacking leg.

Chapter 9

Chinese Kuntao

Indonesia's Punishing Art

In the strictest sense of the word, kuntao is simply Chinese martial art systems and techniques practiced by Chinese peoples who emigrated to Malaysia and Indonesia. However, this very general definition does not fully describe the awesome reputation kuntao has in Southeast Asia. Take, for example, the following story.

The time is World War II. The place is West Java. A detachment of Japanese troops is sent to arrest 67-year-old Liem Ping Wan for operating an illegal radio. Facing his would-be captors, Liem knows that arrest means certain death. Refusing to leave this world without a fight, Liem appeals to his captors' pride: he challenges them to take him—if they can—matching their (Japanese) hand-to-hand skills against his.

Unaware that Liem Ping Wan is a kuntao master, the Japanese soldiers completely underestimate the unimposing figure. Twenty-three Japanese soldiers fall before the twenty-fourth ends the contest with a bullet.

The accuracy of this story—whether there were 10, 15, 20, or 25 captors—is unimportant. What makes this account significant is the fact that a Chinese kuntaoer is the hero. In a country with its own formidable fighters, the report of a kuntaoer killing so many enemy is a testimony to the awesome reputation kuntao has earned.

Americans have had very little exposure to kuntao so it is understandable that, on seeing it, most think it only a little different from kung fu. But to the old masters of Southeast Asia, there is a world of difference. One such master is Willem de Thouars.

KUNTAO'S LEADING EXPONENT

Looking at him, you would not think this slender, gentle-looking man capable of even defending himself, let alone meting out punishment, but beneath his smiling face and disarming manner lie the heart and skill of a kuntao master. De Thouars comes from a family whose martial art heritage goes back to before the turn of the 20th century. His grandfather, great-uncle, father, uncles, brothers, and even his wife, are all martial artists. With that kind of martial art heritage, one would

Figure 228: Willem de Thouars.

have expected de Thouars to pursue his family's art of pentjak silat serak, but that was not the case.

Born in Indonesia, January 11, 1936, Willem de Thouars was the fourth (and smallest) of six brothers. His brothers—all big men—practice the family art, an art that is well suited to their size. Willem, on the other hand, is built nothing like his barrel-chested brothers. Because of his slight build, de Thouars felt that the family art would not work as well for him. Add to this his admittedly rebellious nature, and it's little wonder that Willem chose to travel a different path. Instead of studying the family's system, de Thouars pursued another, but equally respected martial art: Chinese kuntao.

Roots

Kuntao, as taught by de Thouars, traces its origins back to the 19th century and a Chinese gentleman named Li Po Chang. According to de Thouars, Li Po Chang was born in the Hunan province of China around 1830. During his life he studied hsing-i, pa kua, and t'ai chi ch'uan, eventually developing his own system, which he called *po kwa zen*.

After the death of Li Po Chang in 1900, one of his disciples, Lama Darmon, a Taoist priest, became the grandmaster of the system. Lama Darmon was born in China around 1875. In 1912, after changing his name to Liem Ping Wan, he moved to Indonesia, eventually settling in West Java. It was while in Indonesia that Liem Ping Wan developed his system of ch'uan chu shing-i, and it is with this man that de Thouars began his martial art journey.

Willem de Thouars began kuntao training under Liem at the age of 5. Although kuntao is a very secretive art, one kept strictly for those of Chinese blood, Liem broke with tradition and accepted the young de Thouars as his student. He did not do this as a favor to anyone, or to repay a debt; he simply took pity on a frail and sickly child.

Partly from tradition, but more likely because the young de Thouars was so weak, his first six months of training consisted largely of pulling elephant grass and practicing the horse stance. Both exercises may have been necessary to teach the young de Thouars discipline or to test his determination, but the physical exercise they provided also served to strengthen him physically.

World War II saw de Thouars, along with many Indonesians, in Japanese internment. It was during this time that his instructor was killed. However, the death of his teacher did not mean an end to de Thouars' training. Before his death, Liem had already introduced the young de Thouars to three of his "finished" disciples, setting the stage for him to continue his formal training with them.

From 1946 to 1953 de Thouars trained with Tan Tong Liong, studying his internal-external system of que moi shantung kuntao. In 1953, Tan sent de Thouars to William Chen, where he trained until 1954 in external kwantung po kwa zen kuntao. When Chen felt that de Thouars' training had progressed sufficiently, he sent him to the third of Liem Ping Wan's disciples, Buk Chin. Under Buk Chin, de Thouars studied t'ai keh (t'ai chi) and po kwa zen kuntao, completing his training with him in 1956. This, however, was only part of the training de Thouars received during these early years.

In 1949, while still under the tutelage of his kuntao teachers, de Thouars studied sikwitang and kendang silat from Raden Sunario and Mas Atmo. He studied silat with them for seven years. Further, from 1950 to 1953, de Thouars also studied samull petjut silat (a combination of petjut silat and kuntao) from a Muslim priest named Raden Djuran Hadji Samul. De Thouars' formal instruction in these silat systems is directly responsible for some 30 percent of the principles, forms, and techniques he teaches in his system of *kun lun pai, wu kung kuntao, ratu duri silat*. The other 70 percent of de Thouars' system is traditional kuntao.

TRADITIONAL KUNTAO

Unlike many classical martial arts practiced today, traditional kuntao is not taught or practiced exactly as it was fifty or a hundred years ago. This is because the strongest tradition in kuntao is the tradition of change. Initially, I believed that kuntao masters always sought function over form and consciously made changes as needed from one generation to the next. This, however, may not be the case. In *Weapons and Fighting Arts of Indonesia* Don Draeger made the following observation (Draeger 1992, 164):

> Kuntao tradition has it that the master teacher will always teach less than he knows to protect his superior status. Since only the most dedicated and proficient students would be capable of deducing the untaught portion, in time kuntao systems

narrow and stagnate. Only by the application of each succeeding master's additions to the original system can the art perpetuate.

Draeger's observation seems reasonable when we recall how Li Po Chang took what he received and synthesized it into his own system, po kwa zen. Liem Ping Wan, Li's disciple, further refined what was passed on to him into his system of chuan chu shing-i. Liem taught three "finished" men: Tan Tong Liong, William Chen, and Buk Chin. Each, in turn, continued the tradition, expanding the art in different directions. By design or by chance, then, the tradition of kuntao is, undeniably, change.

Kuntaoers honor the contributions of past masters, but they are unwilling (or unable) to blindly preserve outdated and outmoded techniques. Preserving the techniques of the past is a poor idea anyway, since doing so ignores the reality that change and renewal are undeniable and irreversible constants in life—and in fighting.

Adapting to change is the strength of any fighting system. Western boxers respect the contributions of men like John L. Sullivan and Jim Corbett, but no fighter today would even consider practicing their boxing styles. Change, then, is both the tradition and the strength of this formidable art, Chinese Kuntao.

KUNTAO AND SILAT—FUNDAMENTAL DIFFERENCES

Contrasting kuntao and silat is difficult because, to the uninitiated, they often look alike. This is because, like the Indonesian culture itself, considerable intermarriage and melding of the two arts has occurred over the centuries. In the chapters that follow, technical differences and similarities are examined in detail; however, before pursuing that vein, we need to understand the fundamental difference that separates these two arts. A simple analogy illustrates this difference.

Imagine, if you will, two life-and-death struggles: four men fighting—two men on one mountain, two more on another. On the first mountain, high on a cliff, a silat fighter defeats his foe and his adversary falls a thousand feet to his death. On another equally high precipice, the kuntaoer also defeats his enemy. Only the kuntaoer's opponent does not simply fall a thousand feet to his death. Instead, he smashes into the cliff walls every hundred feet or so—all the way down. The fundamental difference between silat and kuntao is like that—both arts are lethal, but with the kuntaoer you are punished in the process, dying many times over.

All of this begs the question, how can two arts be that different—fundamentally different—and still look so much alike? The fact is that both arts benefited from the other's presence, and each contributed in some measure to the other's development. Despite this, the evidence strongly suggests that silat's influence on kuntao was much greater than was kuntao's influence on silat. However, it is a mistake to assume that kuntao's influence on the indigenous Indonesian art is as small as some silat purists would lead us to believe. Silat practitioners, for example, would have made every effort to study kuntao, if only to be able to defend against it. Before considering Chinese influence on Indonesian arts, let's look at how the Indonesian arts influenced their much older Chinese counterparts. Knowing this will help us see how kuntao evolved from classical kung fu, and how those two arts differ.

From Kung Fu to Kuntao—Survival of the Fittest

Although the origins and history of martial arts in China are obscure, undeniably, martial arts have been systematically studied and practiced there for millennia. With so many cultures within China's borders, Chinese martial arts evolved into literally hundreds of systems. However, that great national martial diversity within also had one major drawback: it reduced the need to look without for fresh input. Over time, this meant that although the various Chinese systems and styles were different, the rules of engagement were often the same. Put simply, Chinese practitioners were usually fighting other Chinese practitioners and training accordingly. With their migration to Southeast Asia, however, the rules of engagement changed.

Malaysia and Indonesia were radically different combat environments. Chinese immigrants there no longer faced "civilized" opponents who fought as they did (much as the British discovered during the American Revolution). Now, Chinese martial artists faced a different fighter—fierce men with considerable skill and determination—and with an approach to fighting like none the Chinese could recall.

The problem for Chinese fighters was the very thing they prided themselves on most: their martial art legacy. Because of China's long martial art tradition, its "fighting arts" had, over the centuries, evolved into "martial arts"—complete with ethics and codes of conduct. However, in Indonesia, they were still practicing *fighting* arts. Indonesia was a dangerous place to live, and one did not waste precious training time studying martial arts for such reasons as self-cultivation, self-improvement, or artistic expression.

Another problem was the fact that Malaysian and Indonesian fighters made extensive use of edged weapons. Our use of firearms has reduced the emphasis on edged weapon training in silat today, but this was not the case at all in 16th-century Indonesia. As Chinese martial artists found themselves facing skilled pentjak silat fighters, their skills were seriously tested. The skill of their Indonesian and Malaysian opponents was formidable. Silat fighters were cunning, fast, and lethal. One's life depended on his skill, and techniques that were ineffective were soon discarded. To survive, Chinese immigrants had to return to their art's fighting roots. They were forced to revive—and often rediscover—neglected skills that were long forgotten; hidden now in artistic expression. It was back, then, to the furnaces that originally forged the Chinese arts.

What went into the crucible were the martial skills of two very different cultures: the time-tested skills and theories of classical kung fu and the deadly reality of pentjak silat. What came out was awesome. The fighting art forged from the fire of combat produced a fighter whose determination and skill made him look and fight like an angry hornet among killer bees.

Gone were the flamboyant, stylized, and overly specialized techniques and movements of classical kung fu. Gone as well were the numerous health movements that had become entrenched into what were previously fighting arts. These were discarded in favor of skills that would better preserve one's health (combat can be a very unhealthy experience).

High-powered, high-percentage strikes meant to do the most damage in the shortest possible time replaced those nonessential elements. Elbows from pentjak silat—the most devastating weapon in the empty-hand arsenal—took the place of classical (and impractical) hand strikes. Pentjak silat leg tactics and destructions replaced outdated static stances and methods of movement. Between what was replaced and what was retained, Chinese martial arts moved once again into the realm of fighting arts; what was once kung fu was now kuntao.

Blitzkrieg—Kuntao Style

Among martial arts, kuntao has to rank as one of the most aggressive of self-defense arts. The cardinal rule of this art can be summed up in three words: attack, attack, attack. It is as if there is no such thing as defense; only attack and counterattack. Not that kuntao proposes to be the aggressor or the bully, but if a fight is inevitable, the kuntaoer is prepared to go into it with everything he has. Every block is an attack and every attack blocks or covers the kuntaoer's own vulnerabilities.

Secondary or supplementary strikes fill the space between the major, more obvious blows. These minor strikes go unnoticed by observers because they are so subtle, yet it is their incorporation in the kuntaoer's arsenal that makes his defense synergistic and completely overwhelming. For example, as the hand recovers from one strike to position itself for another, it often disregards the shortest path to its next position, seeking, rather, a path that will allow it to inflict additional pain along its way.

In my analogy illustrating the fundamental or philosophical difference between kuntao and silat,

Figure 229: Silat player slipping the punch.

Figure 230: Silat player's position after slipping the punch.

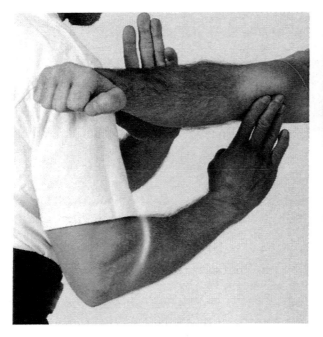

Figure 231: Close-up of shearing hand position.

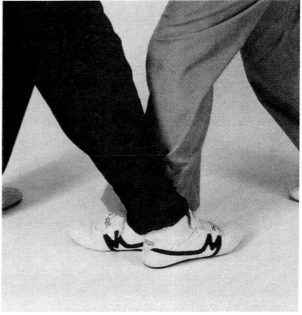

Figure 232: Close-up of silat player's foot placement.

the kuntaoer's mountaintop adversary did not simply fall a thousand feet to his death but, instead, smashed into the cliff walls every hundred feet or so—all the way down. It is a good analogy, but how is this philosophical difference manifested in a fight?

FROM THEORY TO PRACTICE: COMPARING THE TWO IN ACTION

The differences between a kuntaoer's approach and that of a pentjak silat practitioner are visually subtle, but *tactually* significant. Although they may look alike, they *feel* very different. In the sequences that follow, the defense is made against a typical American attack: a right haymaker punch from a left lead. Let's begin with the pentjak silat fighter's defense.

Pentjak Silat Defense: Positioning Is Key

Against a right haymaker punch delivered from a left lead, the silat practitioner redirects his opponent's punch to the right as he slips outside the blow (figs. 229 and 230). Simultaneously, he knifes his hand through his opponent's attacking arm (positioning it for his next move) as he slips his right foot outside and behind his assailant's left (figs. 231 and 232).

Already the silat fighter is in a position to take down his foe. However, before finishing him, the silat fighter uses a glancing blow to his opponent's head (fig. 233) to soften him up and, simultaneously, position him for the finish. Because his opponent is badly pretzeled, a clothesline strike to the head (fig. 234) easily takes him down.

Figure 233: Softening up his opponent.

Figure 234: Taking opponent off his feet.

Figure 236: Digging his knuckles deeply into his opponent's elbow.

Figure 235: Kuntao Master Willem de Thouars defends by attacking his assailant, ripping his knuckles through his opponent's elbow.

If the cardinal rule in kuntao is attack, attack, attack, then the cardinal rule in silat is position, position, position. Looking back at the silat practitioner's technique, you can see that throughout his defense his goal was to gain superior position over his opponent. The silat fighter used what I call positional strikes, not to injure his opponent as much as to distract and annoy him until he was in just the right position to lower the boom (see figs. 231 and 233). When the silat fighter was ready to finish his opponent—to knock him off the proverbial cliff—he had everything in position to do it convincingly and almost effortlessly.

Now let's look at how a kuntaoer might approach the same attack and what he does differently. In this sequence, kuntao master Willem de Thouars demonstrates the kuntaoer's defense.

Figure 237: Recoiling in pain, the assailant moves off his intended line of attack.

Figure 238

Figure 239: Trapping attacker's lead leg.

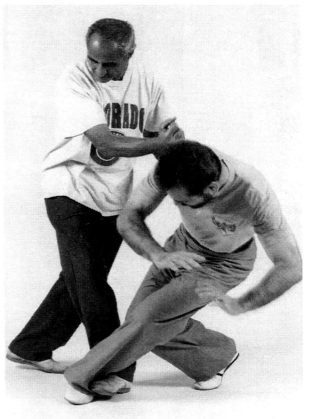

Figure 240

Kuntao: Direct and Brutal

Defending the same attack, the kuntaoer's response is much more aggressive. Believing that pain and punishment are the best deterrents to aggression, the kuntaoer immediately attacks his assailant. Driving his knuckles deep into the tender inside of his assailant's right elbow (figs. 235 and 236), the kuntaoer causes his attacker to depart from his intended line of attack (fig. 237).

To most observers, this initial response is only a little different from the silat fighter's; however, the difference between the two is both tactically (the purpose and procedure) and tactually (the feel) very different. Tactically, the kuntaoer attacks his opponent and uses pain to make him miss. The silat fighter made his opponent miss by moving off his opponent's line of attack while simultaneously deflecting his blow. Tactually, the kuntaoer immediately gives his opponent something else to think about—

reason to regret his foolish act. Outwardly subtle differences like these account for most of the confusion surrounding contrasts between kuntao and silat.

Continuing, the kuntaoer now presses his stunned attacker. Using classical pa kua ch'uan footwork, the kuntaoer traps his opponent's near leg (figs. 238 and 239) and, while applying pressure to that leg, slams his right fist and wrist into his assailant's neck (fig. 240). The punishing blows coupled with a simple, but effective leg lock send the kuntaoer's opponent to the ground. With his legs twisted from the kuntaoer's effective use of the leg lock, the attacker is especially vulnerable to having them broken as the kuntaoer stomps all over them as he follows him down.

Figure 241   Figure 242   Figure 243

The kuntaoer might choose to apply the principle of adhesion while standing up. Smashing his fist into his attacker's arm as in Figures 235 and 236, the kuntaoer maintains contact with his assailant by moving in and keeping his right arm against his assailant's (fig. 241).

As if climbing up his attacker's arm, the kuntaoer pulls himself to his opponent with his right hand as he slams a left forearm into his neck and head (fig. 242). Simultaneously—and unbeknownst to his assailant—the kuntaoer slips in a left leg lock inside and behind his opponent's near left leg. Sticking to his assailant as he applies pressure with his left leg, the kuntaoer pulls his opponent toward him as he jams his thumb into his eye (fig. 243). Unable to fight or flee, the hapless assailant is brutally punished.

These two techniques give you a glimpse into kuntao's aggressive, punishing fighting style. Adhesion and application of leg-locking techniques (the same ones shown in leg-locking drills four and one, respectively) are just two of the principles used in this kuntao defense.

Kuntao's Uncertain Future

As a fighting art, kuntao's future seems uncertain. This is because the kuntao and silat that are practiced today are not the kuntao and silat our teachers learned. The practice of classical kuntao is discouraged in Indonesia because it is too violent (death was all too often the result of challenges), and traditional silat was, for many years, shunned in the Dutch homeland for the same reason. It seems that the study of classical kuntao is considered detrimental to the prevailing social and political climate; kuntaoers simply scare bureaucrats. Tae kwon do and karate are considered less violent than classical kuntao and traditional pentjak silat. As such, they are socially acceptable. And, according to the old masters, their influence has turned the once-potent Chinese and Indonesian arts into little more than pastels—watered-down mixtures of kuntao, silat, tae kwon do, and karate.

When queried about the status of kuntao in his country, a young Malaysian friend and fellow martial artist replied that he had never even heard of it. Kuntao there is either lost forever or taught so secretly that most people are completely unaware of its existence. According to mustika kweetang silat Master Jim Ingram, the Chinese still keep their kuntao to themselves. Willem de Thouars, a student of the art and teacher with more than a half-century of experience, says, "Kuntao is a basic Chinese fighting style that is hardly recognized anymore . . . everything has become kung fu, wushu, or kenpo."

Very few know kuntao. Fewer still teach it. To the uninitiated, it is often mistaken for either pentjak silat or kung fu, but it is neither of them. Kuntao is a devastating art that brings together the best of both worlds: Indonesia and China, pentjak silat and old Chinese kung fu.

Because of its no-frills, no-flash, no-nonsense aggressive style, its punishing attitude, and its unwavering requirement for well-practiced fundamentals, kuntao holds little interest for the masses. The Indonesian government has no interest in promoting it and has in the past even tried banning its practice. If kuntao survives at all it will be due to the efforts of a dedicated few: those who refuse to compromise kuntao's philosophy and demanding training methods. Kuntao may never be a commercially viable art, but for the serious martial artist, if you can find it, it is one you will not want to pass up.

C all it *kuntao*, *ch'uan fa*, or *kempo*—however you pronounce it, each of these words comes from the same Chinese characters, and all have been translated variously as "fist law," "fist rule," "fist way," and "the way of the fist." According to those knowledgeable in these things, the word *kuntao* is made up of two simple words: *kun* and *tao*. *Kun*, literally translated, means, "a game played with the hands." *Tao* means way, rule, or law. The literal translation of these two simple words, then, is "a game played with the hands," and "rule, law, or way."

With most languages, however, literal translation is woefully inadequate in rendering an accurate meaning. Take, for example, the case of the computer program that attempted to translate Russian technical journals into English. Since it could only translate literally, it completely missed the mark when it translated the Russian term for "hydraulic ram" into "water goat." "Fist way" and "fist law" also miss the mark, although not so dramatically. If we move beyond the literal translation of "rules of a game played with hands" [rearranged] we come to "boxing principles." Fist law, fist rule, fist way, and so on are all acceptable, but boxing principles better captures the characters' real meaning.

However, for the best sense-for-sense translation, one last refinement is necessary. Substitute the word "fighting" for "boxing." We do this because to the Western mind boxing carries a hands-only connotation, where in Asian martial arts it includes both hands and feet. Substituting "fighting" for "boxing" removes that "hands-only" impression, making "fighting principles" the best translation of this term. As a kuntaoer and one interested in learning principles, I find that fighting principles best captures the essence of the art known as kuntao.

Chapter 10

Jurus

The Flowers and the Fruit

In karate, kung fu, and tae kwon do, part of the training focuses on "forms" practice. Called *kata* in Japanese, *kuen* in Chinese, and *hyung* in Korean, forms training involves following prearranged patterns of movement—like choreographed shadowboxing. Although a few are two-man sets, most are practiced solo. In pentjak silat, the closest thing to forms are often called *jurus* (*djurus*) or *langkas*.[1]

As a form, a *juru* is practiced in one of two ways: for public display or for combat. In public, the practitioner reveals only the art's flower (*kembang*). There he displays the art's extraordinary beauty and grace. However, he does this in an expression that hides the movement's underlying martial intent and lethal potential. Only in serious practice—

that is, practice for self-defense and combat—does the silat practitioner expose his art's bittersweet fruit, or *buah*. Little is hidden in the *buah* because life and death depend on it. Pentjak silat *jurus*, then, are Indonesia's fighting forms.

So seriously and intensely are the *jurus* practiced, and so closely are they tied to their combat application, that conflicts between expert silat practitioners are often settled by simply having each fighter perform his *jurus*. Observing his opponent this way affords the prospective combatant the opportunity to determine the other's skill and consider the cost of a real fight. To some, revealing one's combat skill is unthinkable; given the fact that fights between silat experts often ended in death, however, such an approach seems prudent. For example, had Saddam Hussein known the strength of the forces arrayed against him, he might have pulled out of Kuwait of his own accord and saved the lives of countless Iraqi soldiers. There is reason behind this curious Indonesian custom.

In this chapter, you see *jurus* from pentjak silat as they are chained together and practiced as a form.[2] Although the form is shown in its entirety, it is impossible to explain every movement in detail. For this reason, only three sequences are shown in application against opponents, and then, only one of the sequences' many possible interpretations is given. This is because, although *jurus* are often taught as specific self-defense techniques, they are only taught this way to make it easier for the student to grasp. Their real purpose lies in teaching principles of movement. For example, a movement that looks like an upward block is just as easily executed as a forearm strike to the neck; without a target, their motions are identical. The direction a technique takes, then, depends on how the movement is interpreted.

The form you will see is performed using a mixture of *kembang* and *buah*—flower and fruit. This is done to give you a glimpse of both the *juru's* artistic expression and its combat potential.

Punctuating the blow-by-blow are two reccurring terms: *Indo-cat* and *Indo-bow*. A right Indo-cat is an Indonesian variation of the classical cat stance where the right foot is forward and placed flat on the ground. This differs from the classical cat stance most Western martial artists recognize because the front foot of the Indo-cat is flat on the ground. In the classical cat stance, the front foot touches the ground either with the toes or on its ball.

A left Indo-bow is a left-foot-leading front, forward, or bow stance. In this Indonesian variation, the rear knee is bent, and, as with the Indo-cat, both feet are flat on the ground.

In my instructions, rather than always using the word "stance," as in, "turn and seat into a horse stance," I will shorten most of them to "turn and seat into a horse." Also, although we will begin the form with a frontal picture, changes in orientation are necessary to give you the best view. Orientation and direction are indicated by degrees and points of the compass. A clock is also used, but its orientation is vertical, as if hanging on a wall. To reduce the confusion that changes in orientation cause, a reference line (running east to west) is used to indicate north. For example, when the silat player faces north, the line will be in front of him like the top of the letter "T." When he is facing south, the line will be behind him. Eastward and westward direction will have it alongside. Finally, I have taken the liberty of dividing the form into sections titled as follows: salutation, first series, second series, third series, etc., and closing. These divisions are provided only for ease of transmission. In reality, because the *jurus* teach movement rather than technique, what looks like the end of a technique in one interpretation may not be the end in another. Again, the divisions used here are only for helping you follow the sequence of events. That said, let's begin with a form called *juru satu*.

JURU SATU: THE FIRST FORM

Juru satu means simply "set one" or "first set." It is the first form taught by my instructor. Other instructors may teach a similar form as their first form, or a completely different one.

Figure 244: The beginning position.

Figure 245: Salutation from the front.

Figure 246: Salutation from the side.

Figure 247: Praying hands—from the front.

Figure 248: Praying hands—side view.

Salutation

Begin in a neutral stance with your feet together and your arms at your sides (fig. 244). Drop your weight over your left leg and slide your right foot forward to a right Indo-cat. Simultaneously, bring your right fist up to a position in front of your right shoulder. Your fist (with its palm toward you) is placed beneath your open left hand (figs. 245 and 246). This position represents the fighter's preparedness.

Both hands join, forming praying hands directed to the front (figs. 247 and 248 show frontal and side views). This position signifies the fighter's desire for peace. Should peace prove impossible, however, then the silat fighter has already demonstrated his steel.

First Series

From the praying hands position, explode into a right Indo-bow with your right hand transforming to a palm-up fist (figs. 249 and 250 show frontal and side views). Exploding into the stance means that you seat suddenly into the Indo-bow—as if launched into your position. In this explosion, both feet move at once. Your right foot moves forward a short distance as your left foot moves back an equal span.

As you explode into the right Indo-bow, your right hand forms a fist that circles or rolls inside your left palm—forward,

Figure 249: The right Indo-bow—front view.

Figure 250: The right Indo-bow—side view.

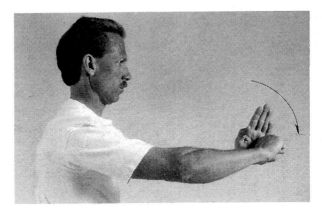

Figure 251: Right hand forms a fist and rolls forward.

Figure 252: Right fist rolls down and back.

Figure 253: The right hand returns as a fist.

down, and back up—transforming into a palm-up hammer fist pressed into your left palm (figs. 251 through 253).

Simultaneously reaching forward with your left hand while pulling back your right fist, allow your shoulders to rotate clockwise about 15 degrees (fig. 254). Now, pivot left 90 degrees and seat smartly—as if exploding—into a horse. As you seat, drive your right forearm into your make-believe opponent's chest as in Figure 255. (Your forearm strike is simulated by striking against your complementing hand in a pincer-like

Figure 254: Extending the left hand.

Figure 255: Horizontal elbow strike.

movement. In application, a shearing elbow strike is used, but in absence of a real target, you use the pincer action.)

Turn back to a right Indo-bow and execute a reinforced, open-hand right outward parry (fig. 256); your left palm reinforces the parry. Unlike a classical outward parry, which terminates with the defender's elbow six or more inches apart from his ribs, this parry is completed by pulling the arm back in tight. That is, the bulk or meat of the defender's forearm is pressed against his ribs (fig. 257). However, without pausing at the end of the parry, you immediately execute a reinforced horizontal right punch (fig. 258), retracting the punch immediately after the blow, as shown in Figure 259. (Like the parry, the punch terminates with your right forearm pressed tightly against your ribs.)

Figure 256: Reinforced outward parry.

Figure 257: Forearm pressing against ribs.

Figure 258: Reinforced right punch.

Figure 259: Punch terminates with the player's forearm pressed against his ribs.

Figure 260: Switching from right punch to parry.

Figure 261: Outward parry.

Figure 262: Parry complete. Ready to strike.

Figure 263: Reinforced left punch.

Switch hands and execute a reinforced, open-hand left outward parry as in Figures 260 through 262 (your right hand reinforces the parry). Again, without pausing at the end of your parry (which you completed with your left triceps pressed against your left ribs), strike immediately with a reinforced left horizontal punch (fig. 263). This time, however, do *not* retract your punch. Although your next move is an advance, you will move to the punch instead of reining the punch back to you.

Second Series

From your right Indo-bow, step forward (north) with your left, advancing into a left Indo-bow. As you advance, open your arms, pulling them back toward your face, as in Figure 264. (We call this movement "spreading eagle's wings.") As if clearing a front bear hug and smashing the neck, continue the motion, circling your hands forward and bringing them together, driving an inverted (palm up) left hammer fist into your right palm (fig. 265).

Reaching forward with your right hand as you pull back your left fist (fig. 266), allow your shoulders to rotate counterclockwise about 15 degrees. (Think of this as tightening the spring.) Pivot right and explode into a horse, simultaneously slamming your left forearm into your make-believe opponent's chest, as in Figure 267. (You again simulate the forearm strike by striking against your complementing hand in a pincer-like movement.)

Turn back to a left Indo-bow and execute a reinforced, open-hand left outward parry (fig. 268);

Figure 264: Spreading eagle's wings.

Figure 265: Left hand hammers into right palm.

Figure 266: Extending the right arm.

Figure 267: Left horizontal elbow strike.

Figure 268: Reinforced outward parry.

Figure 269: Parry stops with the left forearm pressed against the ribs.

Figure 270: Reinforced left punch.

Figure 271: Retracted punch stops with the forearm pressed against the ribs.

your right palm reinforces the parry. Remember, this is a tight move, and you complete the parry with your forearm (not your hand or wrist) pressed against your left ribs (fig. 269).

Without pausing at the end of the parry, immediately execute a reinforced horizontal left punch, as in Figure 270, retracting the punch after the blow (again, with the forearm pressing against your ribs, as in fig. 271).

Figure 272: Right outward parry.

Figure 273: Parry stops with right forearm pressed against the ribs.

Figure 274: Reinforced right punch.

Switch hands and execute an open-hand, reinforced right outward parry (figs. 272 and 273); your left palm reinforces the parry. Without pausing at the end of your parry, immediately fire off a reinforced horizontal right punch, as in Figure 274. (Here again, you do *not* retract your punch because you will follow it in as you stick to your imaginary opponent.)

Figure 275: Left hand reaches out.

Figure 276: Advance with a right vertical elbow.

Figure 277: Continue to a strike to the groin.

Third Series

You should now be in a left Indo-bow, facing north. Starting your next advance with a small stutter-step, you retract your left foot a few inches, then advance your right foot north to a right Indo-bow. Simultaneously, your left hand reaches forward and your right hand retracts (fig. 275). As your right foot advances to the right Indo-bow, you drive a right vertical elbow strike to the front (fig. 276). Simulating contact, your elbow strikes your left palm. Immediately, your elbow circles up, around to the back, and down, returning as a right palm strike to your imaginary opponent's groin (fig. 277).

Figure 278: Strike-left intercepts the punch, then . . .

Figure 279: . . . the left hand strikes and follows the clock.

Figure 280: Seating with a downward hammer strike.

Shift your attention to your left and execute a strike-left combination to the northwest (fig. 278). As your left hand makes the second, displacing motion of the strike-left combination, have your right hand continue its initial motion and let it travel counterclockwise from twelve o'clock (where it intercepted the punch) to six o'clock and back to twelve o'clock. (If this is confusing, imagine you are facing a large standing clock.) As your right hand travels the circuit, your left hand follows it; only your left hand traverses the twelve to six o'clock counterclockwise path, stopping at the six o'clock position.[3] From its twelve o'clock position, your right hand hammers straight down into your left palm as you seat into a horse, as in Figures 279 and 280. (Remember, your left hand had stopped at the six o'clock position, directly in front of your groin.)

Figure 281: A low-line knee strike.

Figure 282: Kicking backward.

Figure 283: Block-right as you pivot right 180 degrees.

From this position—you are in a horse, facing northwest—pivot left to a left Indo-bow and drive a low-line right knee into and through both of your hands, as in Figure 281. (Your hands will strike your knee and continue a little past it.) With your right knee still in the air, kick it straight back—low and to the east (fig. 282). Then, pivot sharply right 180 degrees, turning to a right Indo-bow with a strong block-right combination (fig. 283).

Before beginning the fourth series, let's look at one possible interpretation to the third series (figs. 275 through 283). Remember, the third series begins with the defender in a left Indo-bow, facing north. Avoiding an attack, the defender parries the incoming right punch (fig. 284), then advances, stepping through and driving a vertical right elbow into his assailant's ribs, as in Figure 285. (Maximum power is delivered to the target by timing the strike with the advance to the right Indo-

Figure 284: Deflecting opponent's punch.

Figure 285: Elbow strike to opponent's ribs.

Figure 286: Right palm strikes opponent's groin.

Figure 287: Strike-left.

Figure 288: From strike-left to putar kepala.

Figure 289: Second attacker dumped at defender's feet.

Figure 290: Right knee to assailant's head.

Figure 291: Block-right against the third attacker's jab.

bow.) From the elbow strike, the defender's elbow whips up and back (possibly glancing off his assailant's head or face) and returns as a right palm strike to the groin (fig. 286).

A second attack now comes from the defender's left front (northwest). Using a strike-left combination, the defender checks the incoming punch (fig. 287). Completing strike-left and pulling his assailant's right arm inside and down (from twelve to six o'clock), the defender executes a move called *putar kepala* or "turning the head" (fig. 288). Pulling the assailant's head down and in spins him like a top and dumps him at the defender's feet.

"Playing the drum," the defender slams a right hammer fist down into his assailant's face (fig. 289). Finishing, he drives his right knee into his downed opponent (fig. 290), then wheels quickly around, just in time to use a block-right combination against a third attacker (fig. 291).

This should give you some idea of the potential these fighting forms have. But let's resume our walk through the form with the fourth series.

Figure 292: The position you were in at the end of the third series.

Figure 293: Left hand to a position beneath the right armpit.

Figure 294: Right foot retreats as your left hand slides forward.

Fourth Series

The fourth series begins with the 180-degree pivot, turning to a right Indo-bow with a strong block-right combination, as you saw in Figure 283. At this point, you are in a right Indo-bow facing east (fig. 292).

Slipping your left hand (palm down) beneath your right armpit (fig. 293), step back with your right foot to a left-leading open horse.[4] As you withdraw to the horse, your left hand slides beneath and along your right arm as if clearing a grasp from that arm[5] (fig. 294).

From your left-arm-forward (extended) position,

Figure 295: Right and left horizontal punches.

Figure 296: Note the change in perspective.

fire off a quick right and left horizontal punch combination[6] (fig. 295). Immediately, the left hand drops down and back to a position directly in front of the groin, where it claps against the right palm (the fingers of both hands point down). As the left hand claps with the right, you seat deeper into your left open horse (fig. 296).

Turning it left 45 degrees, stomp your left foot (fig. 297). This movement begins a 270-degree left turn to the north.[7] During your turn, your right foot travels all the way around to the north, stopping with you in a right Indo-cat (facing north). As you turn, both of your hands angle upward 45 degrees and forward, stopping when you reach your north-facing position (figs. 298 and 299).

Facing north in your right Indo-cat with your arms up, drop to a low right-foot-leading crouch,

Figure 297: Left foot turns out, beginning the 270-degree turn to the north.

Figure 298: Right foot follows the left, turning 270 degrees north.

Figure 299: Facing north.

Figure 300: Seating.

Figure 301: Jumping front kick.

Figure 302: Edge palm strike north.

bringing both of your hands down to a position in front of your right shin; your arms will almost encircle your bent right knee (fig. 300). Immediately spring back up with a jumping right front kick (fig. 301). In midair your shin strikes against your right palm. (Striking your palm terminates the kick and limits its height.) You recover in a right Indo-bow with a right-edge palm strike to the north, as in Figure 302. (As your right palm strikes forward, have it shear against your retracting left palm—like clapping hands with your left hand slapping your right palm as it goes forward.)

This is a good place to stop and look at one possible interpretation to the action that has just taken place in the fourth series. This sequence begins with the defender wheeling around just in time to execute a block-right combination against a left jab attack, as shown in Figures 303 and 304. (These positions are the same ones you saw in figs. 291 and 283, respectively). Stepping back with his right foot into a left open horse, the defender executes a modified strike-left combination[8] (fig. 305), followed by a quick right and left punch combination (figs. 306 and 307).

Figure 303: The position you were in at the end of the third series.

Figure 304: Block-right against the third attacker's jab.

Figure 305: Left palm strikes your attacker's face.

Figure 306: Right punch to the body.

Figure 307: Left punch to assailant's face.

As the attacker drops his right arm to cover his ribs, the defender traps his hand or arm, clasping it between his hands, and pulls him forward. The pull is effective because the defender seats deeper into his horse as he draws his assailant in (fig. 308). Before his opponent can recover his balance, the defender brings a rising right inside forearm against his neck or head, violently whipping him up and back (figs. 309 and 310). This use of whiplash, coupled with the defender's turning advance to the north, throws the attacker around like a rag doll.

Figure 308: Pulling your attacker down, then . . .

Figure 309: . . . whipping him back up, and finally . . .

Figure 310: . . . whipping him back down again.

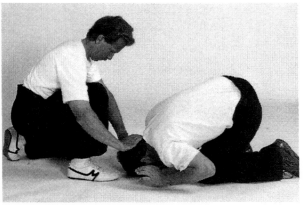

Figure 311: Smashed onto your knee.

Figure 312: Slammed into the dirt.

Dropping straight to the ground, the assailant is either dashed over the defender's right knee (fig. 311) or slammed into the dirt (fig. 312). If the latter is the case, then the defender may leap up—over his downed opponent and onto (or away from) the next threat.

Again, this interpretation is what I call an *E pluribus unum* interpretation; that is, one of many that are possible. Contrary to the way forms are taught in other systems, where a given sequence is always taught to have a specific application, in silat, forms are primarily movement forms. As such, a given sequence can have several valid interpretations.

Fifth Series

Your recovery from the jumping front kick placed you in a right Indo-bow with a right-edge palm striking north (refer to fig. 302). Remember, as your right palm thrusts forward, it shears against your left palm as it retracts.

Turn left 180 degrees to a left Indo-bow. To make such a turn work, both of your feet must make a slight adjustment. Your left foot will turn counterclockwise a few inches, pulling the foot to your left (east), followed by the right foot turning and moving a few inches to your right (west).

As you turn, execute a right inward (right-to-left) monkey-hand strike (fig. 313), followed by a left outward (also right-to-left) monkey-hand strike, as in Figure 314. (The left outward strike flows from beneath the preceding right inward strike.)

The two preceding strikes are followed by two more: right and left inward monkey-hand strikes (figs. 315 and 316). The sequence of strikes is as follows: right inward, left outward, right inward (all three moving from right to left), and, finally, left inward (left to right). The final left-to-right is a classic example of whiplash.

You are now facing south (note the reference line is behind the player). Retract your left foot a couple of inches, then advance (south) with your right to a right Indo-bow. As you step into the Indo-bow, your hands come together in front as if executing a double-hand ear-slap (figs. 317 and 318). Keeping your left foot in place, execute a

Figure 313: Right inward (right-to-left) monkey-hand strike.

Figure 314: Left outward (right-to-left) monkey-hand strike.

Figure 315: Right inward (right-to-left) monkey-hand strike.

Figure 316: Left inward (left-to-right) monkey-hand strike.

sempok—step behind your left leg and sit down with your legs crossed, as in Figure 319. This seated cross-legged posture is a classical Indonesian ground sitting position (you saw this in the Introduction). As you sit, both of your hands come to a ready position directed south. Although this position may seem vulnerable, this is the most defensible of all Asian ground sitting positions.[9]

Figure 317: Advancing south . . .

Figure 318: . . . to a double palm slap.

Figure 319: Right foot steps back (behind the left) to seated position.

Figure 320: Rising from seated position.

Figure 321: The hands cover and clear as you rise.

Sixth Series

Rising from your seated position, you move your right and left hands in a rolling action—right forward, left over right, then right over left (figs. 320 and 321). With the final right over left, you are standing with your right leg kicking southwest. Simulating contact with a target, your kick strikes your right palm (fig. 322). Completing the kick, you remain standing in a right crane stance (fig. 323).

Figure 322

Figure 323: Recovering after your right kick.

Figure 324: Rising left wing-elbow strike.

Figure 325: High elbow strike southeast.

Figure 326: Right hand rolls forward, clearing.

Figure 327: Left hand rolls over your right.

Figure 328: Kicking south-southeast.

Figure 329: Recovering in a standing left crane stance.

Put your right foot down at about shoulder width in front (south-southwest) and execute a rising left wing-elbow strike (fig. 324). Follow that with a high horizontal left elbow strike to the southeast (fig. 325).

Follow the left (southeast) elbow strike with a right-over-left and left-over-right rolling hand motion, similar to the one before (figs. 326 and 327). With the final left hand, you are standing and kicking southeast with your left foot. Here, too, simulating contact with a target, your kick strikes your left palm (fig. 328). Completing the kick, you remain standing in a left crane stance (fig. 329).

Figure 330: Left fist (palm up) strikes into your right hand.

Figure 331: Hacksaw through the left hand.

Figure 332: The same position as Figure 331, only seen from the east to provide a better view of the action.

Figure 333: Draw back, simultaneously slapping your right hand into your left.

Put your left foot down about shoulder width in front (south-southeast) and drive a left inverted fist (palm up) into your right palm (fig. 330). Retract your left foot a few inches, then advance (south) with your right to a right Indo-bow. As you step into the Indo-bow (fig. 331), your right forearm (palm up and hand open) hacksaws through your left palm. (Imagine hacksawing up through a collarbone.)

Note that the fighter's position in Figure 332 is exactly the same as in Figure 331, only the perspective has been switched to reveal more detail. Draw back to a right Indo-cat as you bring your right hand (palm down) crashing down in front, slapping your left hand, as in Figure 333. (Turn your hips and shoulders 15 degrees to the left—almost due south—as your right hand slaps your left.)

Figure 334: High vertical backhand strike (or block).

Figure 335: Right backhand strikes low through the left palm.

Figure 336: Shearing right palm striking south.

Continuing, your right hand returns south as you turn your shoulders and hips back. From the slap through your left hand, your right hand circles to a high vertical backhand strike (fig. 334) and finally down to another backhand strike low (through your left hand), as in Figure 335. Shuffle forward (south) to a right Indo-bow with a shearing right palm striking high, as in Figure 336. The shearing effect is simulated by having your right palm (palm down) strike your left hand, which is palm up.

Before concluding the form, let's look at one more application of the movements

Figure 337: A right hacksaw-forearm strike into the opponent's neck or collarbone.

Figure 338: Pulling the assailant down, whipping him forward.

presented in Figures 332 through 336. This defense begins with the defender moving inside his attacker's right punch and driving the back of his right forearm into his opponent's collarbone or neck (fig. 337). After shoving his attacker back, the defender whips him forward, pulling him down, keeping him off balance and on the defensive (fig. 338).

Before his opponent can recover, the defender whips back, standing his assailant up once again by striking him in the face with a right backhand (fig. 339). Letting his left hand slip up his attacker's right arm to his shoulder, the defender now executes a neck-wrenching shearing palm, pulling his foe's right shoulder toward him as he drives his face in the opposite direction (figs. 340 and 341).

Figure 339: Standing the attacker back up.

Figure 340: The left hand slips up to the opponent's right shoulder as the right hand prepares to strike.

Figure 341: A neck-wrenching shearing palm.

Figure 342: Whirling around to face attack from the rear (north).

Figure 343

Figure 344

Closing

Pivot left 180 degrees as you execute a high left open-hand block (fig. 342). Step forward (north) with your right to a right Indo-cat. Simultaneously, bring your right fist up to a position in front of your right shoulder and beneath your open left hand, as in Figure 343. Both hands now come together, forming "praying hands" directed to the front (fig. 344). Again, this signifies the fighter's desire for peace. Should peace prove impossible, however, then the silat fighter has already demonstrated his ability to do battle.

* * * *

It is not the purpose of this chapter to teach you a form—even a basic one—from pentjak silat. All claims to the contrary, no one learns a martial art from a book. More than 100 photographs were used to demonstrate this form, and still, there was much that simply could not be shown. However, what is presented here should give you some appreciation of the combat application that lies beneath the artistic expression of every Indonesian *juru*. To those with the eyes to appreciate them, the *jurus* of pentjak silat are beautiful. But only those who understand the principles the *jurus* contain also recognize how deadly they really are.

NOTES

1. I say "the closest thing to forms" because, in the strictest sense, *jurus* refer to hand sets and *langkas* refer to leg sets. Moreover, *jurus* are usually practiced as a single set, as in *juru* number 16, much like the Japanese practice a *waza*, or single technique. However, it is when the *jurus* are strung together that most Indonesian instructors recognize the similarity between their *jurus* and *langkas*, and what we call forms and kata. In this light, they often refer to their "forms" as simply *jurus*.

2. Note: In its strictest definition, a *juru* is a single technique. *Jurus* is the plural form of *juru*. Saying that pentjak silat *jurus* (collections of individual techniques) are forms begins to confuse things. For that reason, I will refer to the entire prearranged, chained-together collection of individual *jurus* as simply a "form." I will continue to refer to the individual techniques within the entire set as *jurus*.

3. Your hands travel at opposing positions on the clock. That is, when your right hand is at twelve o'clock, your left hand is at the six.

4. An open horse stance is a regular horse stance, weight evenly spread on both feet, but instead of the feet being parallel, the lead foot is turned out a few degrees.

5. The operative words here are "as if clearing" the arm. Clearing the arm is only one of several possible interpretations for this movement.

6. Only the left punch is shown here.

7. 270 degrees indicates how far the right foot travels in its arc (the left foot serves as the pivot point).

8. This is a "modified" strike-left, because the second (left) hand extends by traveling beneath the right. In a normal strike-left, the left hand travels over the initial right.

9. Attempt to go down to the seated defender and you enter the proverbial "tiger's den"; attempt to kick him and he captures your leg. Without a doubt, you would prefer to remain standing against your opponent, but if you have to be caught sitting on the ground, this is the best position.

Chapter 11

Silat Versus Kuntao

In *Weapons and Fighting Arts of Indonesia* (Draeger 1992), the following question is raised: "Has a pentjak silat fighter ever met a kuntao expert, and if so, what was the result?" People being what they are, the obvious answer to the first question is yes. As for the result, well, let's just say that despite silat's significant influence on the Chinese arts that were brought to Indonesia, there is at least one case where the Chinese art of kuntao was a major contributor to the development of a system of silat.

A TALE OF TWO MASTERS

At an appointed time and at a location known only to the combatants, two men— one Chinese, the other Indonesian—squared off. Deadly in their skills, they both came prepared to fight. Kuntao expert Kwee Tang

Kiam faced a fearsome pentjak silat fighter named Mustika. Although such contests frequently ended in death, this one gave way to life, for the result of this contest was the birth of a new system of pentjak silat, a system that would be called kweetang or kwitang silat.[1]

Muslim practitioners claim that Mustika, a Muslim priest or *kjai* (pronounced KI-EE), defeated the Chinese drug peddler Kwee. Moreover, Mustika's victory over Kwee validated both the *kjai's* skill and the effectiveness of the Indonesian art over the Chinese kuntao. The defeated Kwee, recognizing the *kjai's* skill (and his mercy, for sparing his life) turned from his evil ways, converted to Islam, and became a disciple of his new master, Mustika. Some suggest that Kwee eventually married Mustika's sister, thus creating a familial bond between them. Somewhere in all of this, the *kjai* chose to name his system of silat after his former foe—or so goes the Indonesian version of the contest.

The Chinese, as you might expect, tell a very different story. Kuntaoers agree on the combatants involved (Kwee and Mustika); however, they dispute the claim that Kwee was a drug peddler and that the *kjai* won. Kwee, they say, was an honest merchant (and kuntao master), and it was he who defeated the infamous, drug-dealing Mustika. Further, they insist that the development of kweetang silat is the result of master Kwee marrying an Indonesian (possibly the *kjai's* sister) and teaching his native (Chinese) art to his new (non-Chinese) relatives and neighbors. Why else, they ask, would an Indonesian system be called by a Chinese name?

What is certain from these two conflicting stories (and is undisputed by both sides) is that at one time a Chinese kuntaoer named Kwee fought a pentjak silat practitioner named Mustika. What can be supposed from the two accounts is that each combatant was highly skilled and each respected the other's ability (if not before their fight, certainly after). It is also possible that after testing each other's skill, they may have even trained together. In any case, the result of their contest is a system of pentjak silat that bears the Chinese name kweetang.

KWEETANG TODAY

Although known informally as kweetang silat, the system's formal name is mustika kweetang silat, in honor of the two men responsible for its development. Mustika kweetang silat was brought to the United States by Jim Ingram in 1961. As amiable as he is skillful, Guru Besar (Chief Instructor) Jim Ingram is the foremost Dutch-Indonesian authority in this art in the United States.

Born in the west Java harbor city of Cheribon on November 13, 1930, Jim Ingram began his martial art training when he was 8. However, Ingram did not learn his art from his father. Ingram's father, Jimmy Ingram, a local police chief and a very capable martial artist, declined to teach his children the art he knew: pukulan.

By Ingram's account, his father was a "rough guy" (understandable for a police chief in that part of the world) who felt that he was not the best one to teach his children. Realizing, however, that one did not survive in pre-World War II Indonesia without some serious martial art training, Ingram's father turned to a man whose skill was beyond question. He asked William Loreo, a *djago*, to teach his son. A *djago* was a local champion of sorts. Like the town gunfighters from the American Wild West, *djagos* were men of considerable reputation. While many respected and sometimes revered them, others—doubtless with good reason—feared them.

According to Ingram, a *djago* was a "protector from areas that he has to take care: from prostitutes, bicycles, parking lots, stores, pickpockets, what have you." *Djagos* even worked, from time to time, with the local authorities. When, for example, some important person's briefcase was stolen, the police might ask the local *djago* to retrieve it or bring in the individual who stole it.

Although Ingram denies that his teacher sold protection, William Loreo did accept money and gifts for providing same. Here is how Ingram describes his teacher: "He made his living from sponsorship. People put money in an envelope and give it to him for his help. When a *djago* needs things, people give it to him."

Having never met a *djago*, I cannot describe one with certainty, but to my American mind the description given of a *djago* sounds remarkably like a Dutch-Indonesian version of the Italian Godfather—a sort of benevolent Mafia don. In any case, William Loreo was a man of considerable skill and reputation, and the one whom Ingram's father entrusted to teach his son.

William Loreo was skilled in pukulan, tjimande, kuntao, and kweetang silat. In the Indonesian tradition, he took the best of the arts he learned and distilled them into a system that Ingram says would be formally called tjimande mustika kweetang pukulan. Although Ingram prefers the shorter name of mustika kweetang silat, he still teaches techniques from all three systems: mustika kweetang, tjimande, and pukulan. In fact, when asked to show three techniques that exemplify the art and system he teaches, Ingram chose one from mustika kweetang, one from tjimande, and one from pukulan.

Figure 345

Figure 346

A Mustika Kweetang Silat Technique

In this mustika kweetang silat self-defense technique, Guru Besar Jim Ingram slips his attacker's right punch. Simultaneously, in a scissor-like action, Ingram delivers a back-knuckle strike to the soft underside of his opponent's upper arm (fig. 345). Before his opponent can react, recoiling his arm from the first blow, Ingram advances on his foe, driving a sharp punch into his upper thigh (fig. 346).

Destroying his opponent's mobility and weakening his desire to fight, Ingram digs right and then left elbows into his attacker's nearest leg (figs. 347 and 348).

Figure 347

Figure 348

Figure 349

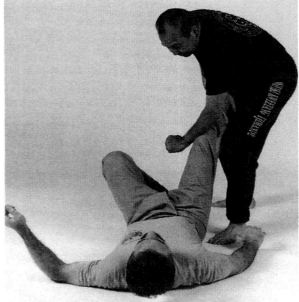

Figure 350

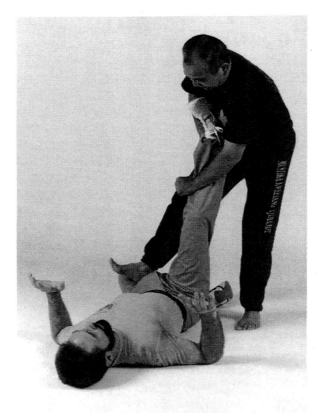

Figure 351

Figure 352

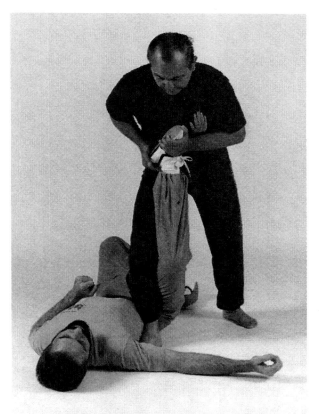

Figure 353

Figure 354

Grabbing his attacker's near leg, and using his own left arm as a fulcrum, Ingram pulls his attacker's leg out from under him, violently throwing him to the ground (figs. 349 and 350).

Before his opponent can recover, Ingram plants a right heel-kick firmly into the inside of his left leg, just above his knee. This prevents his opponent from using his left leg to mount a counterattack (fig. 351). One quick strike to the groin ensures that Ingram can safely step over his downed attacker to finish him (fig. 352).

Stepping over and placing his right foot alongside his opponent's body, Ingram is now in a position to twist his hapless foe's ankle counterclockwise (fig. 353). With his opponent's leg twisted outward, Ingram drops his weight on the trapped leg. This crumples the leg, crushing the attacker. From this position, Ingram is able to finish his assailant with blows to his head (fig. 354).

Pukulan

In this pukulan[2] technique, Guru Besar Jim Ingram slips inside his attacker's right punch with a simultaneous right hand right-to-left parry and a quick left vertical punch to the face (fig. 355). One or more additional blows may be used to soften up the attacker. Here, Ingram follows his left punch with a right (fig. 356).

With a preparatory two-hand chop to the sides of his

Figure 355

Figure 356

Figure 357

Figure 358

Figure 359

Figure 360

Figure 361

Figure 362

Figure 363

Figure 364

Figure 365

Figure 366

attacker's neck (fig. 357) or a double ear slap, Ingram punishes the attacker and simultaneously positions him for his next move (fig. 358). Ingram now pulls his attacker's head down into a rising left knee (fig. 359). From the knee-to-the-head (above), Ingram drops to a kneeling stance, again smashing his attacker's face onto the anvil formed by his right knee (fig. 360).

Rotating his opponent's head counterclockwise, Ingram slams a downward right elbow into the side of his attacker's head or neck (fig. 361). A simultaneous chop to the throat and chop up against his attacker's nose completes the technique (fig. 362).

Tjimande

Because mustika kweetang silat has tjimande roots, Ingram shares this next self-defense technique from that system. In this defense, Ingram begins by stepping off his opponent's line of attack, slipping the incoming left jab with a right inward parry (fig. 363). His left hand is already positioned (below his right) for his next move. After slipping the initial attack, Ingram now advances on his opponent, placing his left leg inside his assailant's left leg (fig. 364). Ingram says that although he uses his left *fist* here in striking his opponent's upper arm, the hand would normally be open in a pure tjimande technique.

A quick right to the left ribs or kidney causes his opponent to recoil his trunk, dipping his head toward Ingram (fig. 365). Taking advantage of the reaction he just set up, Ingram uses his left hand to feed his opponent's left arm to Ingram's left, allowing him to twist his opponent and simultaneously strike him with a rising right knee to his back (fig. 366).

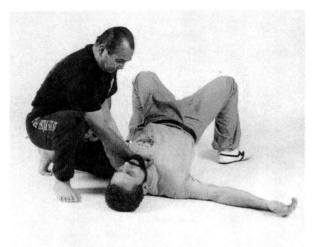

Figure 367

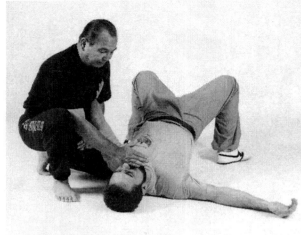

Figure 368

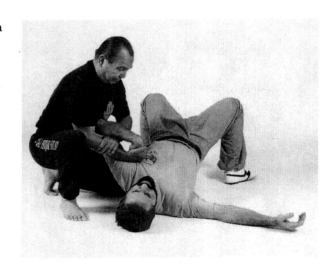

Figure 369

With his assailant's left arm immobilized in an upward armbar, Ingram drives a right backfist down onto his opponent's throat (fig. 367). "Playing the drum," Ingram softens up his attacker with one or more open-hand blows to the face (fig. 368).

Because the attacker's left arm is trapped, Ingram says that the defender can easily switch the armlock to one that uses a gooseneck against the wrist (fig. 369).

SMILES FROM THE PAST

Although they might both laugh at the conflicting accounts of their art's origin, I think that both Kwee Tang Kiam and the *kjai* would smile broadly at how far the art they started has spread. *Djago* William Loreo can also take pride in the accomplishments of his pupil, Jim Ingram, and at the honor Ingram always gives him.

Mustika Kweetang Silat is an excellent example of Indonesian inventiveness, influence, and adaptability. Silat is one of the world's most effective fighting arts. So effective, in fact, that it significantly influenced the Chinese arts that were brought to the island nation—no small feat. Finally, silat's adaptability is nowhere more clearly seen than in the evolution of this system of pentjak silat—a system that bears the Chinese name kweetang.

NOTES

1. *Kweetang* is also spelled *kwitang.* However, the system Jim Ingram learned is spelled *kweetang*—the colonial spelling.
2. Colonial Dutch spelling for this word is *poekoelan.*

Chapter 12

Magic and Mysticism

Magic: *Noun*—The art of producing a desired effect or result through the use of various techniques, as incantations, that presumably assure human control of supernatural agencies or forces of nature.

Mystic: *Adjective*—Having the nature of, or pertaining to, mysteries known only to the initiated; of occult character, power, or significance. *Noun*—A person who claims to attain, or believes in the possibility of attaining, insight into mysteries transcending ordinary human knowledge, as by immediate intuition in a state of spiritual ecstasy.

* * * *

Tell another martial artist that you study pentjak silat, and half the time you are asked some question regarding the magical, mystical, or spiritual side of the art (much, I suspect, like the questions fielded by ninjutsu practitioners). There are, in fact, pentjak silat teachers who claim to have magical power, both in Indonesia and in the United States. There are also individuals who claim no such power themselves but swear that it exists, for in visits to Indonesia they have felt it (Wilson 1993, 2:15). Still others—teachers with many years in the art—seem to practice the art at the highest level without so much as a mention of magic. What, then, is the prospective student of pentjak silat to make of all of this? Does one need magic to really master silat? In a word, no.

Although I am aware of the fact that in some quarters magic plays a significant role in silat, I was not exposed to that side of the art as part of my study and training. This lack of exposure is due at least in part to my having been taught by Dutch-Indonesian teachers, rather than by native Indonesians. As young students in Indonesia, my instructors were taught by their Dutch and Indonesian relatives, as well as by nonfamilial Indonesian and Chinese teachers. However, like myself, they were not taught the religious or mystical aspects of these arts. One wonders why. If Dutch and

Carried away in a trance.

Dutch-Indonesian students were as zealous for silat as it appears, why didn't they also pursue the magical/mystical side of these very formidable arts? To understand the reasons behind Dutch nonparticipation in this area, we need to know something about Indonesia's religious legacy.

INDONESIA'S RELIGIOUS LEGACY

Since before the time of Christ, tales have been told, often through music and dance, of the mythical past when numerous and often terrifying gods lived among men. The ancients of Indonesia were animists—people who believed that spirits, both benign and malevolent, ruled their world. Posing as men and beasts, these spirits possessed powers well beyond mere mortals. Because the spirits often possessed men, they were to be both feared and revered. To this day, the warriors and heroes of that era are immortalized in myth and lore.

Some are revered for their struggle against the often oppressive spirits. Others are remembered because they were empowered by them.

Hinduism

Spiritually, Indonesia is especially fertile ground. Widespread in the archipelago before the 14th century, Hinduism came to Indonesia more than a millennium ago. This religion, with its vision of a world populated by a pantheon of gods, was quickly embraced by many. Moreover, because of Indonesia's animist past, her people proved especially susceptible to Hinduism's esoteric Tantric traditions.

Today, only 2 percent of Indonesia's people are Hindu, but Indonesia is still immensely proud of her Hindu heritage, and the religion still thrives on the island of Bali. There the gods of the Hindu pantheon—some half human, half animal in form—are still worshipped and revered.

Islam

Despite Hinduism's historical role and great influence, Islam, introduced to the islands some 600 years ago, has replaced it among the majority of Indonesians. Some 85 percent of Indonesians claim Islam as their religion, making Indonesia the largest Muslim country in the world. Yet, even among Indonesia's Muslim faithful, the power of the ancients survives. Indonesia's physical and cultural distance from Mecca (the holy seat of Islam) made it impossible for that great world religion to resist the island nation's long-standing animist and Hindu traditions. Sufism, the mystical and ascetic branch of Islam that borrows ideas from other religions and philosophies, dominates Muslim religious practices in this distant land. Like the Tantric traditions of Hinduism before it, the mystical side of Islam found fertile ground in paradise. Despite the power of these great world religions, neither was able to fully displace the influence of the ancient animists.

Christianity

In comparison to Hinduism and Islam, Christianity, a relative newcomer to the islands, has played a very small role in Indonesia's spiritual development. Brought to the archipelago barely 400 years ago by European traders and colonialists, Christianity has not made the impact on Indonesian culture that Islam and Hinduism have. Despite the fact that 8 percent of all Indonesians claim to be Christian—a greater percentage than claim to be Hindu—Christianity appears unlikely to influence Indonesia in any measurable way in the near future.

Hinduism, Islam, and, briefly, Buddhism[1] came to Indonesia in the hearts of those friendly to her—by merchants, missionaries, and citizens returning from abroad. This was not the case with Christianity. The Christian faith was introduced by an occupying power. Being subjugated by another power and condemned to live as second-class citizens in their own country left many Indonesians with bitter memories—memories that nullify any appeal that their occupiers' religion may have had.

The social and political climate during Dutch colonial rule has never been a topic of discussion with my teachers. Doubtless, their recollections of Dutch presence in the Spice Islands would likely be very different from those recalled by native Indonesians. However, considering the brutal treatment Dutch-Indonesians received on expulsion from the country they too called home, one can safely say that they also have suffered.

None of this is simply academic information. Knowing the religious background of both native and Dutch-Indonesians is important if we are to understand the opposing positions taken on the question of magic, mysticism, and the art of pentjak silat.

THE EVER-PRACTICAL DUTCH

Pentjak silat is generally conceded to have a strong association with spiritual practices; practices that developed through silat's long contact with animist and mystical Hindu and Islamic religious traditions. It seems, however, that Dutch-Indonesian masters (formerly Dutch-Indonesian students of Indo-Chinese arts) were not particularly interested in those elements.

Of silat's physical and spiritual elements, the Dutch contented themselves with learning only the technical, physical side. This is due in part to their Christian faith. From a strictly religious perspective, the spiritual element inherent in Asian martial arts is largely incompatible with Christianity. This is especially true of pentjak silat with its use of, and intercourse with, spirits. This incompatibility exists because Christianity is, by definition, an "exclusive" religion—not in the sense of excluding people, but in the sense of making an exclusive claim to the truth. This is probably the biggest reason the Dutch were not all that interested in the metaphysical side of the art. Among Dutch practitioners, then, even among those who did not consider themselves particularly religious, the magical elements of the art were not pursued.

Setting aside religious incompatibility, there is another reason why Dutch and Dutch-Indonesian practitioners remained on the physical side of the fence: practicality. To the Dutch, studying magic as a means of self-defense made little sense. Magic for self-defense was considered a waste of time because its effectiveness is, at best, questionable; at its worst, nonexistent. Few Western minds are willing to accept claims of physical prowess without physical contact, and the Dutch are no exception. From both religious and secular perspectives, then, Dutch students were inclined to seek out teachers who, like themselves, also had little time for the magical/mystical side of the art.

Protectionism?

In fairness, however, I must mention that another possibility exists. It is possible that native Indonesian teachers were simply unwilling to share this "dark side" of their art with their "ethnically inferior" colonial overlords. They may have withheld those elements (as was often done by Chinese teachers) because they did not wish to give away the thing they believed gave them power. This possibility is reasonable but, in my opinion, weak, in light of the fact that the Dutch had little (if any) interest in this side of Indonesian arts. Surely, after three centuries in the islands, the Dutch were quite familiar with Indonesian beliefs and the role they played in their martial arts. Any "dark side" instruction they were not given—even when they knew the teacher was holding back—was not something they desired in the first place.

Did native Indonesian teachers hold back any practical physical part of their art to give them an edge? Possibly, but would not their Dutch and Dutch-Indonesian students have noticed the difference between their training and that of their fellow Indonesian students? Martial artists learn as much from their interaction with fellow students as they do from their teachers. Practical physical skills, even if not formally shared, will, as I stated before, be adopted by others. Considering all of the evidence, then, it seems more likely that the Dutch simply were not interested in the mystical and magical side of pentjak silat because, as far as they were concerned, it added nothing to the art's highly potent physical skills.

In any case, since independence from the Netherlands in 1949, Indonesia has experienced a resurgence in the teaching of these spiritual elements. In recalling the success of Indonesian fighters in their struggle for independence, many Indonesians believe that the difference between their success or failure was the result of pentjak silat's peculiar magical practices—specifically the use and manipulation of an inner force called *tenaga dalam*.[2] This inner force is similar to the Chinese chi in some respects, but its embodiment is distinctly Indonesian.

CHI—WITH A TWIST

Although emphasis on the spiritual elements in pentjak silat varies from system to system (some teachers avoiding all involvement; others delving deeply into them), all begin with physical training. Self-defense, or *beladiri*, is always taught on a physical level first. Having mastered this, the practitioner may pursue the study and development of inner power or *tenaga dalam*. The titles *maha guru* (master teacher) and *pendekar* (spiritual leader or champion) are often bestowed on those who reach these highest levels of spiritual development. However, spiritual development in silat goes well beyond mere personal inner force and tapping into the energy of the universe. Indonesian spiritual training incorporates supernatural power.

Within the realm of personal physical capabilities, *tenaga dalam* is very much like chi. Using the mind to produce physical healing and walking on hot coals without incident are examples of the power of the human mind. However, it is when one extends this observable and verifiable mental ability beyond the body that one moves into the realm of myth (or, as we shall see, into the domain of the supernatural).

Beyond the medical and purely personal physical uses of chi, some of its proponents claim such things as the ability to injure or disable an assailant without physical contact. Some profess to being invulnerable in combat (like the claims of the Chinese boxers during the Boxer Rebellion). However, because of its shamanist and animist roots, *tenaga dalam* takes the practitioner beyond even this.

Using only *tenaga dalam*—that is, without any physical contact— one is said to be able to kill at great distances, cast spells on enemies, and even read minds. There are also stories of its influence on inanimate objects. Tales are told of silat masters whose *krises* (wavy-edged daggers or swords) rattled in their scabbards in the presence of unseen enemies! Are these reported abilities fact or fiction; truth or myth? Although the answer to that question is the subject of considerable debate, the source of this "power" is not.

Faustian Quest

According to some researchers, this inner power, this "chi with an Indonesian twist," is a direct result of supernatural spirit possession. In an article in *Journal of Asian Martial Arts*, James Wilson wrote of silat practitioners who, on entering trances, behaved as animals, eating offerings of grass and fodder—offerings "often mixed with ground glass." Moreover, if the possessing spirits were dissatisfied with any of this, he noted that the "spirits have been known to keep their human hosts, who then never returned from their state of possession" (Wilson 1993, 2:15). Call it what you will, but Wilson and other witnesses describe this age-old Faustian quest[3] as nothing other than "demon" possession.

For those still willing to do business with spirits, the question remains: Do they get what they bargain for? Can a silat master, using only *tenaga dalam*, disorient or kill an opponent? If empirical evidence is any indicator, then the answer is no. When he asked for a demonstration of the power of *tenaga dalam* on himself, Wilson was told that because he was untrained in its use, he "would face almost certain injury." The only test he was permitted involved blindfolding two of the master's students. The students would, from a distance of approximately 30 feet, strike each other using only their *tenaga dalam*. Without going into a detailed explanation of the students' performance, Wilson sums up the impromptu test in four words: "The students failed miserably." (One can imagine the two students hurling their "inner force" back and forth at each other, producing disjointed, almost comedic, results.)

PRACTICE, PRACTICE, PRACTICE

The use of chi as a method of self-defense has never been proven or verified by established scientific method. *Tenaga dalam*, like chi, is (for lack of better words) an undefinable force or energy that is said to exist in each of us. To use this force, we are told, one needs to have it awakened. From this writer's perspective, the difference between chi and *tenaga dalam* is in who (or what) does the awakening.

Pentjak silat may be studied with or without magic. Even in Indonesia, there are those who use it and those who do not. The Dutch-Indonesian masters I have observed are devastating martial artists without it. Mustika kweetang silat master Jim Ingram, when asked about developing internal energy or chi, answered with the words of his late teacher William Loreo: "When you need it, it will be there—just keep practicing."

The real magic is what average people can accomplish when they work, study, and train diligently. Legitimate masters become masters by doing exactly that: no mysticism, no spirits, no magic—just years of dedication and disciplined hard work.

NOTES

1.   I have not previously mentioned Buddhism. Although globally significant as an Eastern religion, its influence in Indonesia was brief and has all but vanished.
2.   *Tenaga* means force and *dalam* means inner.
3.   "Faustian quest" refers to a 16th-century learned German doctor, Johann Faust, who performed magic and died under mysterious circumstances. According to legend, Faust sold his soul to Mephistopheles (the devil) in exchange for youth, knowledge, and magical power.

Chapter 13

Learning How to Hurt Someone

In a world where violence of any kind is frowned upon, Indonesia's fighting arts must seem as if they come from another, desperate and darker period. They do. How, then, do instructors of these arts reconcile social responsibility and the potent combat skills they share? This question has vexed martial artists for almost as long as fighting arts have been taught. Despite much soul-searching and hand-wringing, it seems that martial artists are no nearer today to resolving this dilemma than their teachers' teachers were in their time.

It is unrealistic to expect, in one short chapter, to resolve an issue about which volumes have been written. However, considering the violent nature of the arts described in this book, some remarks on the subject are in order. Let me begin by recounting a discussion that took place on the Internet.[1]

The whole issue of social responsibility came up when a subscriber to a martial art news group told of a brown belt who had recently used his skill to thwart a would-be mugger. The brown belt and a female companion were heading for their car in a public parking lot. Before reaching the vehicle, the man was grabbed from behind, placed in a choke hold, and threatened with bodily harm unless he turned over his wallet.

Believing that submission was no guarantee of safety—for himself or his companion—the brown belt chose to resist. When it was all over, the mugger received a broken arm for his trouble and was taken away by police. The reporting officer (who had not, by the way, witnessed the attack) told the brown belt that he had used excessive force. The witnesses, however, strongly disagreed, and no charges were brought against the martial artist.[2]

All of this sparked a lively debate among the group's subscribers. More than a few were elated at the fact that at least this time the good guys won. However, a number of others expressed disappointment in both the brown belt's actions and the somewhat jubilant attitude among some of the discussion participants. One individual decried the "he-got-what-he-deserved" sentiment, saying that it saddened him to see so many martial artists rejoicing in an act that resulted in injury to another human being. He recalled Gichin Funakoshi's feelings of sadness and remorse on having to use his skill to restrain a would-be mugger. (The incident referred to occurred immediately after the second world war, when Funakoshi, the father of karate-do, was held up by an unemployed former Japanese soldier.) The "saddened" subscriber went on to say that martial arts are not for self-defense. Rather, he said, they are for self-development and perfection of character.

PERFECTION OF CHARACTER

"Perfection of character." Gichin Funakoshi used those words when he said, "The ultimate aim of the art [karate] lies not in victory or defeat, but in the *perfection of the character* of its participants."

Despite soaring crime statistics, the idea that martial art study is not for self-protection but for self-development and perfection of character is popular among many martial art enthusiasts. One martial art writer (Wingate 1993, 2:16), in an informative article about the ideology of karate-do, argued that "*budo* is the practice of a martial art *for the sake of self-development rather than for combat*" [emphasis added].

Budo may be a way of practicing martial arts for the sake of self-development and enlightenment, and for the instructor teaching children, self-development is a worthy and legitimate training objective; but one does not study or practice pentjak silat and Chinese kuntao for those reasons.[3] Indonesian fighting arts are not martial ways (*budo*[4]). They are fighting arts. They were developed exclusively for self-protection. As such, their instructors make no apology for the fact that they are teaching their students "how to hurt someone."[5]

SOCIAL RESPONSIBILITY

Clearly, this learning-how-to-hurt-someone attitude runs counter to current thinking, but this honest perspective is both refreshing and socially responsible. Instead of telling you that the skill you are learning is for personal, intellectual, or spiritual development, and not self-defense, silat and kuntao instructors tell you up front that this knowledge is, at the very least, dangerous and, at its worst, potentially lethal.

Teaching an individual how to punch, kick, elbow, knee, or slam another person into the dirt, all the while telling them that they are not really learning this to do bodily harm, is hypocritical. Such thinking trivializes the very real danger of the skill imparted, much as playing with a toy gun diminishes a child's perception of the real weapon's potential.

In an effort to justify participation in a violent discipline, some resort to a "but I would never want to do this to anyone" smoke screen. Does this higher-purpose mentality absolve the martial artist from blame when he is forced to use his skills? Saying "I didn't want to break his arm" does not change the fact that I have trained and dedicated many hours learning how to do exactly that.

We are better off admitting that martial arts are "martial," and that martial artists are, for the most part, learning how to hurt their fellow man. That accepted, we might just take more responsibility for our actions, not less.

Personal Responsibility—Not Excuses

How do instructors of fighting arts reconcile social responsibility with the potent combat skills they share? Some may limit their instruction to adults only—neither I nor my instructor, for example, teach children. Others may screen potential students, refusing to train those of questionable character. Beyond that, their approach is much like the one firearms instructors take.

Those who teach firearms use do so with a sobriety and sternness that tells the student, "What we do here *is* dangerous—and definitely *not* to be taken lightly." Because of the danger inherent in firearms training (and their ultimate use), safety and personal responsibility are stressed over and over again. No one in those classes believes that he or she is learning to use the weapon to be a better person. Even those learning it for sport are very well aware of its potential to kill and destroy.

Many enjoy firearms training and practice, but they never lose sight of their subject's potential for harm. Instructors of pentjak silat and Chinese kuntao take the same approach. They enjoy what they do; they even call it play. But they never forget that their goal is knowledge of, and skill in, self-defense—which necessarily means "learning how to hurt someone." Admitting this, they believe, does more to make martial artists socially and personally responsible for their skills and actions than claiming any other purpose for their training ever will.

NOTES

1. The Internet is a worldwide network of computer networks that are connected to each other, providing, among other things, electronic mail, news, and other services. In our case, it was a martial art news group, or bulletin board.
2. This account, as with any unsubstantiated story, should be taken with a grain of salt. However, the root issue it brings to light and the discussion that followed raise important questions.
3. I am speaking of sharing these arts primarily with adults. Teachers of children have additional responsibilities. Namely, to be role models, teaching fair play and sportsmanship, etc. This is true for any teacher of children, regardless of the subject.
4. In Japanese, *bu* means "martial" and *do* means "way," hence the term "martial way."
5. Please note that I said teachers of these arts are teaching their students *how* to hurt people. There is a world of difference between learning *how to hurt* and learning *to hurt*.

Chapter 14

Kun Lun Pai

The Heart and Soul of Willem de Thouars

In the Acknowledgments, I said that credit for this book must be given to my instructor, Willem de Thouars. His broad experience in pentjak silat and Chinese kuntao, coupled with his willingness to introduce his students to other masters of Indonesian arts, really made this book possible. However, the skills, theories, and training methods presented here go far beyond de Thouars' technical instruction. Contributing as much to this work as the technical specifics are the attitude, philosophy, and heart of Willem de Thouars. Those attributes, and their impact on my martial walk, are the focus of this chapter.

• • •

It is no secret that my primary reason for studying martial arts has always been self-defense. When I began training with Willem de Thouars it was for the express purpose of improving and enhancing my self-defense skills—and I was pretty matter-of-fact about that (hardheaded is more like it). I wanted no nonsense, no culture, and no philosophy; just hard-nosed, crash-and-bash self-defense. To Mr. de Thouars' credit, he graciously tolerated my hardheadedness and worked with me as patiently as a Dutch uncle.

As I gained proficiency in the arts de Thouars was sharing, I became increasingly comfortable (and confident) in my self-defense abilities. As the comfort level increased, I began relaxing more and enjoying not only the training but the teacher as well. I found myself learning more than just technical skills, though, for it soon became evident that this man was sharing his heart and soul.

In a close teacher-pupil association, one cannot help learning, if only osmotically, his teacher's culture and personal philosophy (something I previously thought was a waste of time). But de Thouars' philosophy was not some "look at the moon" ideology. It is different—practical; and in a unique way, it contributed significantly to my development and growth as a martial artist.

Having spent considerable time detailing technical specifics, I felt that an entirely different direction was necessary to round out this book. The approach here is more conceptual than concrete. It avoids historical and technical specifics and focuses more on the transcendental aspects of kun lun pai.

When I began studying with Willem de Thouars in 1983, I found myself repeatedly asking, "What is kun lun pai?" My students also wanted to know what it was, since I was sharing with them everything I was receiving as quickly as I received it. I knew I was not studying kun lun pai—I was studying Chinese kuntao and Indonesian silat, but that did not explain the name: kun lun pai.[1]

De Thouars described Kun Lun as a mountainous region in the Honan province of China that was famous for its great fighters. *Pai*, he said, means society. *Kun lun pai*, then, is a society, an association, a brotherhood of men and women who have the dedication and the drive to become martial artists in the spirit of those from the Kun Lun Mountains.[2] De Thouars chose the name kun lun pai to, in his words, "give grace" to his teachers.

While I found his explanation informative, I did not find it enlightening, for it still left my question unanswered. My students knew what they were studying: Chinese kempo, kung fu, and so on. They also knew that our school name, Je du-too, was just that—a name; the name of our school—the Je du-too School of Martial Arts. But kun lun pai was not that kind of name.

I remember bouncing ideas off fellow students of de Thouars—ideas about what I thought kun lun pai was. I remember how, on hearing my thoughts enunciated, I found they were both right and wrong. They were "right" for that time in my training and "wrong" because my vision was too small. I expect my vision is still too small, but the following is how I now answer that puzzling question: *what is kun lun pai?*

WHAT IS KUN LUN PAI?

To describe kun lun pai, I first need to eliminate those things that it is not. For one thing, kun lun pai is not a style. Among martial artists, style has two meanings. For some, it means an individual's personal style; his way of doing, performing, or practicing his art. For others, it is more like a subsystem of a broader art, as in "shorin-ryu stylists."

If one defines style as an individual's personal style, his way of practicing his art, one can argue that kun lun pai is a style. In fact, de Thouars often describes what he teaches as "Bill's backyard." "Bill's backyard" is de Thouars' way of saying that this or that is neither pure silat nor pure kuntao. Rather, it is his way of combining and practicing them both. However, calling kun lun pai a style in that sense of the word is too narrow.

When de Thouars describes what he does as his backyard, he does so out of complete humility. He took what he learned and synthesized it into what works for him, but he never intended it to be an accurate representation of his teachers' arts. It is neither pure silat nor classical kuntao. It is, rather, an amalgamation of the best of both arts and, while this is what Bill does, it does not make kun lun pai a "style."

As far as a subsystem of a broader art, that too is short-sighted. De Thouars trained, initially, in three schools of kuntao and four schools of silat. Of which art is kun lun pai a subsystem? Kuntao or silat? No, we are not kun lun pai "stylists," because kun lun pai is not a style—in either sense of the word.

Kun Lun Pai as an Art

The term "art" is one that encompasses many systems and styles. For example, pamur, tjimande, tjikalong, serak, harimau, sikwitang, and kendang all fall under the art of silat. Likewise, shorin-ryu, ueichi-ryu, goju-ryu, wado-ryu, and shotokan all come under the karate umbrella. Each school, or *ryu*, may have its own distinguishing characteristics, but most martial artists recognize the above Okinawan and Japanese martial arts as karate (versus, for example, jujutsu). Each system or subset, each spoke beneath the umbrella, is not the art itself. Rather, these are differing systems and subsystems within the art of karate. Further, within each system are many masters, each teaching his own version or personal style of the art he practices. So, in this sense, kun lun pai is not an art. The question arises, then: can one call it a system?

Kun Lun Pai as a System

The dictionary definition of "system" is lengthy, but applied to the martial arts I believe it is: an organized set of concepts, ideas, and principles forming a unified whole, including the material presented and methods of training (the operative word here is *organized*).

In this sense, kun lun pai might be called a system, except for the fact that it is not yet sufficiently organized. It has some structure, a rudimentary system of organization, but what exists is insufficient for presentation to, and subsequent assimilation by, Western-thinking Americans; certainly, it is not for beginners.

Willem de Thouars is an extraordinary man who can do some very remarkable things, but he is not, by his own admission, organized. His strengths are his spontaneity, his intuitive movement, and his uncanny awareness of everything around him. A friend of mine said it best when he likened Willem de Thouars to a broken-play quarterback. He said that because de Thouars' improvisations are much more beautiful and more effective than any planned response. (It would be too much to expect such a man to be systematically organized as well.) No, kun lun pai is not yet a system.

Kun Lun Pai—A Philosophy

Perhaps the best definition of kun lun pai is: a way of thinking—much like jeet kune do (JKD). Jeet kune do is a martial art philosophy that teaches that one should look for elements within other martial arts that will complement and enhance the knowledge base the practitioner already has. Jeet kune do stresses the need to constantly pare down, distill, and reduce the knowledge accumulated, making it fit the individual's needs and abilities. The knowledge base from which jeet kune do adepts work is basically the wing chun practiced by Bruce Lee. However, the principle of JKD, the way, or *tao*, of jeet kune do, is applicable to any art.

Kun lun pai is a martial art philosophy. It is based on a mixture of de Thouars' arts, culture, life experience, and unique communication abilities. Like JKD, it stresses making the art, whatever the art, fit the martial artist—not vice versa. The knowledge base kun lun pai practitioners work from is primarily a combination of Indonesian pentjak silat and Chinese kuntao (as practiced by Willem de Thouars). Also, like modern JKD, kun lun pai contains a variety of additional influences, such as fencing, boxing, kenpo, and so on; but kun lun pai has something not found in jeet kune do. It possesses a maturity that only time and experience bring.

The Difference Time Makes

Kun lun pai's maturity comes from more than 200 years of living martial arts experience. Its founder, Willem de Thouars, has more than half a century of broad martial arts training. His brothers (all of whom he has worked with) bring the other century and a half of martial expertise to that mix we call "Bill's backyard." Add to that 200 years of living experience the nearly 200 more years of de Thouars' family martial arts tradition (which includes the DeVries family lineage as well), and you have some idea of the knowledge base de Thouars works from.

This matrix of centuries of living experience and ancestral lineage is unique among martial artists. This is especially evident when one considers that many of us today (martial artists with two or more decades of experience) are just now discovering concepts that de Thouars can remember as having been around for scores of years. One does not have to be a rocket scientist, then, to see the difference that time makes.

Bruce Lee's jeet kune do was the result of his 19 years of martial arts experience (making him a relative newcomer), and although he was analytical, innovative, and brilliant in his ability to cut to the heart of the matter (philosophical or physical), he still only trained for 19 years. (One can only imagine what a mind like his might have accomplished given another 20.)

Lee applied his analytical mind to his martial arts to understand not only what he was doing but also why it worked and what, if anything, could be done to improve it. If we were speaking of automobiles, I would describe Lee's as a Formula One racing machine—possessing an engine of less than two liters in displacement, yet developed to its fullest potential.

Looking under the hood of Willem de Thouars' machine, one finds quite a different engine. His is an eight-liter monster—a stock car engine with unimaginable raw power, limitless potential for refinement, and adaptability to practically any martial art. Like Lee, de Thouars has tuned his eight-liter monster into a machine perfectly suited for him. But unlike Lee, de Thouars passes on to his students a much bigger engine—one offering more raw potential from which to work and more possibilities as well.

Although de Thouars prefers an unstructured teaching style, he does realize the need for some foundation. Kun lun pai, while maintaining the personality of its founder, is, in one way, structured. Three forms—*juru satu*, *juru dua*, and *langka tiga*—loosely form the foundation; but beyond these, everything else de Thouars teaches falls into the realm of electives. Uncle (as he prefers to be addressed) has such a depth of knowledge from which to draw that after a student has learned the required forms (the basics), he simply makes recommendations, suggesting electives for the student—electives he feels best match the student's individual personality and ability.

TEACHING KUN LUN PAI—WHAT TO AVOID

It is important that we do not commit the sin of teaching "traditional" kun lun pai. I say this because the history of kuntao (again, one of the two primary arts taught in kun lun pai) is one that encourages change. As a teacher, de Thouars continues that tradition, and one need only observe each of his senior students to see how that "tradition of change" has been passed on.

Each of de Thouars' senior students, when asked to demonstrate, for example, *juru dua* or *langka tiga*, would perform the same basic pattern, but with some obvious differences. Some of the differences de Thouars allows because of the student's individual ability and personal style, but an equal number of differences are a direct result of the time intervals between each student's receipt of the specific form. To a man, each student says, "Uncle taught it to me this way," or "When I learned it, he did it like this." The point is that each student received his form differently.

Some of the differences are because of the student's perception of what Uncle taught him, rather than what he actually taught (a universal communication problem). However, the main reason for the differences rests with de Thouars himself. Willem de Thouars is, without a doubt, a true martial arts master. He is also a student—a student with more than half a century of training and experience, but a student nonetheless. Because he is always learning, what de Thouars teaches changes over time; it has to.

This kind of change is evident in my own training and teaching. My students will tell you that what I teach now is considerably different from what I taught just a few years ago. (Fortunately, they also say it is better.) The same is true for all instructors (those who continue to train and study, that is) whether they admit it or not.

I have met, for example, individuals who trained with Bruce Lee when he was in Oakland, California. I have also met those who studied with him when he was in Los Angeles. Although there are similarities in what members from each group teach, there are also differences. The same is true for the students of Willem de Thouars.

The forms de Thouars teaches today are basically the same as they were 10 years ago, but they are not exactly the same; there are differences. Students who originally learned their forms in the seventies manifest some not-so-subtle differences from those who learned them in the eighties. The forms de Thouars teaches today have changed. They are not as they were 10 and 20 years ago, and they are probably a long way from the versions he received from his instructors. This is partly by design and partly human nature, but in either case, its acceptance is the essence of kun lun pai.

Except for the recent infusion of some practical application (and Hollywood innovation) by Steven Seagal, aikido is a well-preserved and, in my opinion, dying art. This is because in an effort to preserve the teachings and techniques of O-sensei Morihei Ueshiba's original art, his followers have changed aikido from a once viable self-defense system to one that is practiced primarily for physical and spiritual culture. Kun lun pai teaches self-defense arts. To so preserve the techniques and forms of Willem de Thouars to the point that they are no longer applicable for self-defense would be to commit the greatest injury to his name and the teachers he so honors.

The Task at Hand

The task of American instructors in kun lun pai is to implement a structured teaching methodology that facilitates the sharing of the principles of kun lun pai to Western-minded Americans. That requires walking a fine line between structuring (and strangling the life out of) kun lun pai and letting it run so loose that anyone can claim he teaches it.

I said earlier that "kun lun pai is not yet a system." If we are successful in our task, we will be one giant step closer to moving kun lun pai from a philosophy to a system of martial arts based on the principles of self-defense found in the Chinese and Dutch-Indonesian martial arts. To do this, each of us must resist efforts to standardize kun lun pai forms into a single version. This is critical because once we standardize, we will lose a wealth of knowledge.

Individualized Instruction, Individual Insights

With each student, de Thouars provides an application and interpretation of the techniques and principles in a given form that is custom-tailored to the individual's physical traits and ability. The same application might be different, or completely absent, from the way he teaches the same form to another. Standardizing the forms among his students would be a mistake, for it will result in a loss of more principles than it will preserve.

It is impossible for one teacher, possessing such a depth of knowledge, to pass all of his knowledge and skill on to a single student, even if the pupil trains with him all his life. Such a task requires many students. Because of this, each of us must retain the forms, drills, and techniques we received *as we received them*—not literally, freezing them in time, but sharing them with each other and explaining our understanding of the material we received. We must balance this "preservation" of our individual insights with an emphasis on keeping the timeless qualities and principles of combat that always apply in self-defense—even though that may require some changes by us. What do I mean by that? How does one both preserve and change?

Teaching Timeless Principles

One of the strengths of de Thouars' knowledge is that the fighting principles he teaches are not limited to the prevalent techniques of the day. His techniques work because he knows so well the human body's unchanging dynamics. The techniques work whether the man you face is in a left lead or a right; whether he is large or small.

For example, the silat principle of gyroscopic rotation is effective and timeless because it works on a principle that has not changed and will not change—namely, that one can resist force in only one direction at a time. The principle of gyroscopic rotation, then, is timeless. It worked a hundred years ago, and it will work 100 years from now. Obviously, without some preparatory action to reduce a height disadvantage, an individual five feet tall will have difficulty applying this principle to a man six foot three, but the problem is not with the effectiveness of the principle; rather, it is with its misapplication. Properly applied, the principle is effective and remains timeless.

Holding timeless principles as the goal and adapting them to those things that do change—cultural differences and preferences—while preserving the "play your own song with it" philosophy de Thouars so often emphasizes is the challenge. That will require looking for and isolating those unique patterns of movement found in kun lun pai and migrating existing skills to a level where those movements are effectively and smoothly incorporated. This pattern of searching, recognition, isolation, and systematic application is now, and will continue to be, our main method for the integration of the timeless principles woven throughout the fabric of kun lun pai into the arts that we will teach.

I said "the arts that we will teach" because I believe that, if anything, de Thouars has taught me that a martial art is, by nature, dynamic. It is forever evolving. To remain effective, a martial art must change to meet the challenges presented by new weapons, new tactics, and each new generation of fighters. Because of that, the techniques and forms taught in any school cannot be "cut in stone." What we teach today and what we will teach tomorrow is more than just a philosophy; it is a process. This is the tradition of kuntao, and it is a tradition that Willem de Thouars has faithfully passed on to us. May we, his students, be as faithful in our transmission of this tradition to our students as he was to us.

What Cannot Be Taught

Finally, we come to what, I believe, is beyond our capabilities as students and instructors in kun lun pai, namely, the passing on to our students of Bill's essence—his heart and his culture. When I say Bill's culture, I am not simply talking about Indonesian culture: life-style, diet, dress, and so on. What I am addressing is different for two reasons. First, intellectual or head-knowledge of any culture is little better than no knowledge at all. Second, and more important, de Thouars' background and culture are not pure Indonesian; nor are they contemporary Indonesian—personally, culturally, or martially.

Head-knowledge of Asian masters and their cultures has been sought by Americans for decades. One need only observe the lives of many American *budoka* to see this. Some have, for example, attempted to emulate Japanese life-style and culture in an effort to grasp the secret of their teacher's heart. But such pursuit is like the man who eats Japanese food, wears Japanese clothes, and lives in Tokyo in the hope that this will make him Japanese. Not only is it impossible to become Japanese this way, but to pursue such a goal is to miss the mark completely.

Even if one could assimilate his teacher's culture, it would not work with de Thouars. This is because his cultural roots no longer exist. De Thouars is not Indonesian, but Dutch-Indonesian; and

Dutch-Indonesian culture is nearly extinct. Dutchmen are no longer intermarrying among the Indonesian population today. This is because the Dutch (and their "half-breed" children) were long ago expelled from Indonesia (that is Indonesia's loss). Western and Eastern thoughts and ideas, strengths from both worlds, are no longer being brought together to make an even stronger whole. Even the martial arts of silat and kuntao are weaker for it. Classical kuntao is banned in Indonesia as too violent, and traditional silat is shunned in the Dutch homeland for the same reason. Even the silat that is practiced in Indonesia today is not the silat that de Thouars learned. Tae kwon do and karate are considered less violent and, therefore, socially acceptable. Their influence has in some cases turned the once-potent silat into a watered-down and diluted mixture of silat, tae kwon do, and karate. The culture that produced men like de Thouars, and the arts they practice, no longer exists.

This makes de Thouars (and all Dutch-Indonesians of his generation) unique in our world—again, personally, culturally, and martially. Moreover, just as de Thouars cannot give us the essence of his teachers (like his religious Muslim silat teacher, Haji Samul, or his opium-smoking kuntao teacher, Buk Chin), neither can we give our students the essence that is Uncle. What makes Bill the martial artist he is are the culture from which he came and the circumstances under which he lived, studied, trained, and fought. How can one pass that on to his students?

We can share Bill's "tricks," as he calls them. We can teach the principles and applications that make him so effective. We can even pass on his stories and experiences. But we will never be able to have them feel his energy, his intensity, and his passion for his art.

After close association with Bill for more than a decade, I am just now beginning to know him and to see, albeit faintly, those things within him that make him unique. Some who came to Bill simply for credentials believe they are teaching kun lun pai—and think they know the man well enough to teach his art. They are wrong on both counts. Those individuals have settled for head-knowledge and missed the heart and soul of kun lun pai completely. It is impossible for anyone to learn Bill's art, or anyone else's for that matter, from seminars, videotapes, or casual contact, much less to know and understand the man himself. Such knowledge is possible only from long and close personal contact. As difficult as it will be for me, and the others who have trained with this man, to convey to our students the essence that is Willem de Thouars, it will be impossible for those whose contact with him has been little more than conversational.

The Lion's Heart

If pressed to identify one thing that makes Willem de Thouars unique among martial artists, I would have to say that it is his willingness to fight, with everything he possesses, regardless of the legal or physical consequences. What do I mean by that?

We have become such a "civilized" and litigious society that it is unusual for an individual to invite another to "step outside" to settle their problems. It is even more unusual for them to "take care of business" right then and there (forget stepping outside). A criminal might "take care of business," but he will probably sneak up on you later, catching you from behind. De Thouars, on the other hand, will meet you head-on. One would find Bill doing everything possible to avoid conflict, but once the line has been drawn, one would find him equally committed to action. There is no "I'll only wound him" thinking. There is also no need to worry about him doing something behind your back.

One more thing and I will close. There is one more, equally significant, thing that makes Willem de Thouars unique among martial artists; I mentioned it in the Acknowledgments: his humility. Never have I heard masters of his caliber genuinely acknowledge the fact that another was a level above themselves. De Thouars has. Further, he even gives grace to those who have abused his friendship and attacked his name. He may not be pleased with their actions, he may not wish to have further dealings with them, but he will always be the first to acknowledge their skill and ability as martial artists. Such humility is unique; but then, that is why he is a master.

NOTES

1. In November 1993, because several unqualified individuals were claiming to teach kun lun pai, Willem de Thouars renamed his system wu kung kuntao-petjut kilap silat and made Stewart Lauper's Progressive Martial Arts his headquarters.

2. It is argued that the belief that the Kun Lun Mountains are famous for its fighters may be an erroneous mixing of truths. There is a range of mountains in China known as the Kun Lun Mountains, and there is also a mountain (singular) in China's Honan province noted for its fighters. However, the two are on opposite ends of China. The Kun Lun Mountains are in western China, north of the Tibetan plateau. The mountain in the Honan province noted for its famous fighters is the Song Mountain (Song Shan) on which the Shaolin temple (Shaolin si) stands. However, China is a very large country, and no individual, Chinese or otherwise, can claim complete historical knowledge of such a vast and ancient land. Furthermore, most myths have some basis in fact, so what we have remains largely one historian's word against another's. In any case, the intent for the name kun lun pai is that it represents a brotherhood of men and women who have the desire, dedication, and drive to become martial artists in the spirit of these great warriors—and this does injustice to no one.

Epilogue

Since ancient times aromatic spices from the Far East have been in demand by peoples of the East and West. The Moluccas (today a province in eastern Indonesia called Maluku) have long been famous for cloves, mace, and nutmeg, and were a primary source of spices in the East Indies.

Overland transport of spice from Indonesia to China and Arabia was hazardous and expensive, but the financial rewards for those willing to take the risks were enormous. When large-volume, seaborne trade developed, the "Spice Islands," as they came to be known, attracted both Eastern and Western colonial powers. Indian, Arab, Persian, and, lastly, European traders sought ever-increasing control over the East Indies.

Today the leading exports of the Moluccas are forest products and copra, but to some, the name "Spice Islands" still fits. To knowledgeable martial artists, Indonesia is still the world's largest producer of spice—martial spice, that is. I hope that *Indonesian Fighting Fundamentals* has given you a taste of that spice.

We've looked at tactics, techniques, and methods of movement found in Indonesia's predominant fighting arts: pentjak silat and Chinese kuntao. The purpose, however, was not merely technical specifics. The real purpose was to help you recognize, understand, and assimilate each art's underlying principles. Learning even the best techniques without a thorough understanding of the underlying principles is self-limiting.

Learning techniques without understanding their foundational principles leaves the martial artist ill-prepared when facing new situations and tactics. Fighting is dynamic. It changes with each generation, locale, and situation. Without an understanding of fighting principles, every change, every new situation will require a new technique. On the other hand, well understood and drilled principles result in spontaneity and adaptability—the keys to victory in personal combat.

The principles shown here are in one sense Atlantian. They represent the martial art knowledge of the last generation of Dutch-Indonesian masters. These men are the last of their kind—a dying breed. Born and raised in colonial Indonesia, these children of Dutch and Indonesian unions could train with many teachers. The suspicion that prevented students of one silat teacher from training with another, and the mistrust and hostility that kept Chinese students from studying silat and Indonesian students from pursuing kuntao, was not directed at Dutch and Dutch-Indonesian pupils. Perhaps deference was shown to the colonists and their children in the hope of preferential treatment; one can only guess at the reasons. In any case, Dutch and Dutch-Indonesian students were privy to a vast amount of martial art knowledge and experience—knowledge that was, to all others, closely guarded.

In this book, training methods from other Southeast Asian cultures were freely used to help you learn the principles presented. I make no apology for that. As noted before, one of the keys to success in personal combat is spontaneity. For some, spontaneity is natural. For others, like myself, spontaneity is only learned by rote—doing something over and over, thousands of times. It makes little sense to reinvent the wheel by creating new training methods when good ones are already available.

Mine is not some territorial mission, claiming that this or that is solely an Indonesian innovation; Indonesian arts possess more than enough to crow about without having to steal credit from others. For example, the kilap hand drills presented in Chapter 8 are an adaptation of Indonesian methods to Filipino flow drills. I believe in recognizing another culture's expertise and giving credit to that culture for its contribution. But our highest praise should be manifest in our willingness to credit and use what works well, even if it was developed by another. This "peanut brittle" approach to study honors all contributors in word and deed. Equally important, it significantly improves one's learning ability.

A PERSONAL NOTE

Everyone will agree that Dan Inosanto and Richard Bustillo are truly fortunate to have crossed paths with the late Bruce Lee. However, those two gentlemen both agree that their fortune was doubled because their connection with Lee also brought them together—with each other. A similar set of circumstances exists between myself and the individual who appears with me in many of the photo sequences used in this book. That gentleman is Mr. George Morin: a senior student of Willem de Thouars, and my longtime friend and training partner.

In many ways I have learned as much from my association with George as I have with Bill; in some ways I have learned more. I say that for a couple of reasons. George began his training with Bill when de Thouars was younger and more aggressive in his fighting style. Bill's movement then was less

economical than it is today. This is because he did not have to be as efficient. His vigor and strength allowed him to perform effectively at that time without the requirement for the greater economy that his present age demands. This is true for all full-time, life-long martial artists.

George's movement, like that of a younger de Thouars, is larger and more extended than Bill's is today. I have no doubt that in a real fight, with the adrenaline rush associated with combat, George's moves will shorten and compress, producing the desired economy of movement. Some of Bill's senior students may perform or look more like Bill does today, but George looks more like Bill yesterday.

For myself, this means that those who train to move and look like Bill—as he is now, the Bill we see today—without benefit of their own half-century of experience, may find that in combat, their moves become too condensed. Their movement will likely be shorter than Bill's, so tight, in fact, that their action will be less effective than they expect.

Those training with Bill today need to visualize his movement not as it is now, but as it was before: enlarged. During practice, the student needs to extend and enlarge his own movement, stretch it out, so that like a rubberband, it will spring from and return, when needed, to the place of least tension. To me, George epitomizes a younger Willem de Thouars—graceful and cunning, but with movements large enough to see, and still very effective.

Another reason I have learned as much working with George as I have from studying with Bill is because, as training partners and peers, George and I are freer to question and test the theories each has received from Bill. We are able to compare notes and, where necessary, thrash out a better understanding. This freedom is usually absent in most teacher-pupil relationships.

And "thrash out" is (often literally) what George and I do. We accept the fact that neither of us has all the answers; nor do we always agree with each other's conclusions. There have been, for example, times when my wife has poked her head into a workout session to see what all the yelling and arguing is about! How many times have I said (even in front of my students), "George, that is really pretty, but it only works because he [this student or that] let you do that to him." To George's credit, his response is never defensive. Confronted with our desire to learn, George willingly takes what some would call abuse (a sort of verbal kuntao) to help us all (himself included) discover the truth. Working through our difficulties (with the technical material and with each other) has led to a mutual respect for each other's strengths, perspective, and opinions. The result is a deeper friendship and unbelievable growth for both of us.

I am fortunate to have crossed paths with Willem de Thouars—no argument. His teaching, his knowledge and skill, and his influence have impacted my martial art far more than even he realizes. However, I am equally fortunate to have, by my association with Bill, met and trained with George. In that, I am doubly fortunate.

Bibliography

The Concise Columbia Encyclopedia, 1983.

Draeger, Donn F. *Weapons and Fighting Arts of the Indonesian Archipelago*. Rutland, Vermont, and Tokyo: Charles E. Tuttle Company, 1972. (Reprinted in paperback as *Weapons and Fighting Arts of Indonesia*. 1992.)

Fiorito, Graziano and Pietro Scotto. "Learn by Watching—the Octopus Way." *National Geographic* 184 (December 1992): "Geographica."

The Random House Dictionary of the English Language, The Unabridged Edition.

Shintaku, Shiro. "The Truthful Hand: Keeping the Ancient Ryukyuan Spirit Alive." *Budo Dojo* (Summer 1994): 28.

Wilson, James. 1993. "Chasing the Magic: Mysticism & Martial Arts on the Island of Java." *Journal of Asian Martial Arts* (Volume 2, Number 2): 15.

Wingate, Carrie, Ph.D. 1993. "Exploring Our Roots: Historical and Cultural Foundations of the Ideology of Karate Do." *Journal of Asian Martial Arts* (Volume 2, Number 3): 16.

About the Author

A former marine, Bob Orlando was introduced to the martial arts while on active duty (1961–1964). However, it was not until after he left the service that the flicker of interest kindled there became his consuming fire. Bob began serious study in Chinese kenpo-karate. Later he switched to kung fu, studying under Al Dacascos (then teaching in Denver, Colorado). His training with Dacascos lasted three years, until a back operation made it impossible to continue in Dacascos' high-kicking style of kung fu. It was back to Chinese kenpo, where Bob received his first-degree black belt from Dr. John P. Cochran. Although he has subsequently earned additional rank, he prefers to say that he is a student of the art and leave it at that. "Rank," he says, "is excess baggage. It becomes a hindrance to learning because everyone expects that you already know everything."

Ever a student of the arts, Bob's quest for knowledge has taken him into aikido, iaido, arnis de mano, and eskrima. However, what has impacted him the most are the years he has spent studying Chinese kuntao and Indonesian pentjak silat under Dutch-Indonesian master Willem de Thouars. He studies with him still.

A graduate of a Jesuit university, Bob has written numerous articles for both national and local publication. No longer a tournament competitor, Bob still supports tournament karate and is a founding member and past director of the Colorado Karate Association—a nonprofit organization that works to provide competitors with a positive tournament environment.

Although he does not consider himself a "professional" martial artist (one who makes his living from martial arts), Bob still considers himself a "full-time" martial artist, for he studies and trains constantly. Of his own abilities, he says, "I have many skills, but not because I have any natural talent; I've simply worked very hard to get to where I am today. My fortés are my analytical mind and my ability to share what I know with others. I take the complicated and make it simple. I am a teacher."